ATTACHMENT THEORY

ATTACHMENT THEORY

A Guide to Strengthening the Relationships in Your Life

THAIS GIBSON

callisto
publishing
an imprint of Sourcebooks

CONTENTS

INTRODUCTION

My name is Thais Gibson, and the intention of this book is to teach you how your childhood experiences affect your adulthood relationships—whether they are platonic, romantic, or familial. This book combines attachment theory and a variety of therapeutic techniques to help you identify what attachment style you or your loved ones have and to heal the core wounds that each attachment style may have.

Throughout the years I have spent working with thousands of people in client sessions, seminars, and online programs at the Personal Development School, I have found clear parallels between adult behavior and childhood experiences. This book will combine traditional teachings with knowledge of subconscious patterns to provide tools for deep transformation. The tools throughout this book combine traditional psychological methodologies with new, cutting-edge techniques that I have developed in order to facilitate powerful change.

Throughout this book, you can expect to learn what your attachment style is, what the attachment styles of those around you are, and what steps you must take to become the healthiest version of yourself. It will specifically delve into the underlying habits of Dismissive-Avoidants, Fearful-Avoidants, Anxious Attachments, and Secure Attachments. Moreover, the core subconscious wounds that are associated with those attachment styles will be revealed, and through three primary forms of therapy—Acceptance and Commitment Therapy, Cognitive Behavioral Therapy, and RAIN—I will teach you how to reprogram your subconscious mind.

If you find yourself interested in learning more about yourself and your wellness, I have created a series that offers a wide range of teachings, with courses ranging from Attachment Styles to Discovering Your Unmet Needs.

For more information, visit personaldevelopmentschool.com.

HOW TO USE THIS BOOK

This book is divided into three sections:

1. An introduction to attachment theory

2. An overview of attachment styles

3. The techniques required to heal your attachment style

Within the first section, you will learn the history of attachment theory and understand how it has evolved over time to better encapsulate behavior that stems from childhood experiences. While there is no incorrect way to learn from this book, you will obtain the most value from reading all sections chronologically since each section builds on those before it.

The second section will delve into how attachment styles originate. This section will help you understand what attachment styles you and others in your relationships may have. Once you understand how your style is created, you can begin to understand what unmet needs you may have and how you project certain outdated beliefs onto your everyday life.

From there, the third section will give you the tools that you need to reprogram the outdated beliefs causing chaos in your life and relationships. Each form of therapy will be expanded upon based on my personal research findings to help create real change in your life!

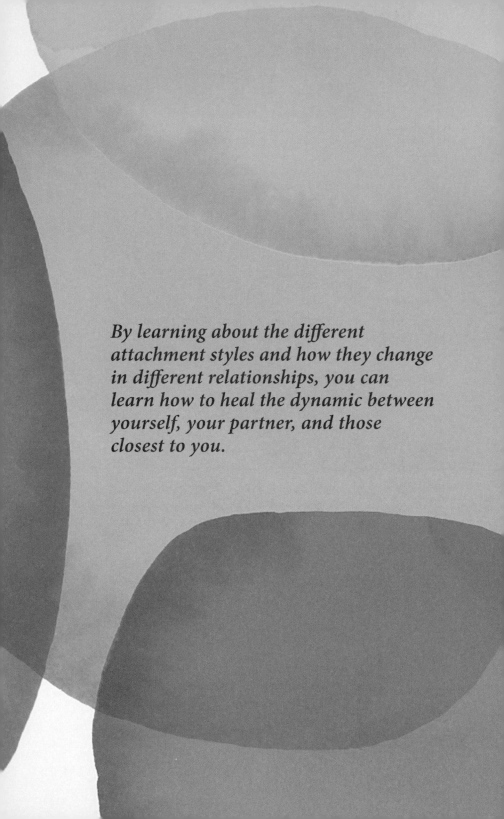

By learning about the different attachment styles and how they change in different relationships, you can learn how to heal the dynamic between yourself, your partner, and those closest to you.

Part 1

ATTACHMENT THEORY

Throughout this book, I will be taking you on an introspective exploration of yourself, your attachment patterns, and the attachment patterns of your loved ones. This will help produce a better understanding of how to move through challenges in relationships, how to transform triggers, and how to more deeply love and understand yourself and others.

The first few chapters will look at what attachment theory is and how our attachment styles impact our day-to-day interactions with others. Numerous studies have shown unequivocal correlations between how someone is parented and the attachment traits that they ultimately express in adulthood. If unhealthy, these attachment styles can be transformed. We can become more secure in ourselves and learn to love and connect in very healthy ways. This book will provide you with tools, strategies, and steps to create healthier patterns and change what is preventing you from reaching your full potential in relationships with friends, family, and romantic partners.

Chapter 1

ATTACHMENT THEORY BASICS

Attachment theory is predicated on the underlying concept that attachment is the primary mechanism within all
our relationships, whether they are romantic, platonic, or
familial. The attachment patterns that impact our everyday relationships can be transformed or exacerbated over
time, depending on our life's circumstances. To learn how
to improve closeness and intimacy in relationships, these
patterns must first be understood.

Our childhood experiences impact the traits that we
express as adults. These impacts are revealed in what we
will refer to as attachment styles. Although there is often
overlap between attachment styles, people *do* have the
ability to shift their attachment style over time. Let's imagine there is a woman named Chen. As a child, her parents
were completely negligent. Due to substance abuse issues,
neither parent was emotionally available or present during
the moments Chen needed them the most. When Chen had
challenges with schoolwork or problems being bullied at
school, her parents did not notice. As a result, Chen came to
believe that in order to survive she had to be self-sufficient.
This belief became a part of her sense of self and was then
brought into her friendships, romantic relationships, and
perpetuated even in her familial relationships.

Chen has struggled with being vulnerable to others
throughout her life because of the vulnerability she experienced as a child of negligent parents. Chen had friends
and romantic partners but never felt deeply connected to

them and couldn't understand why. She didn't realize that her own belief patterns around attachment caused her to subconsciously avoid getting too close to others in order to not feel hurt again.

This is an example of just one attachment pattern that consistently occurs yet is rarely understood by the individuals themselves. It is essential for Chen to understand how this happens so that she can transform what is creating loneliness and acting as a barrier to human connection.

In this chapter, you will learn more about the origins of attachment theory and what attachment styles exist. When you are equipped with these tools, you will have the foundation to begin transforming your relationships.

What Is Attachment Theory?

Attachment theory is the study of how childhood experiences with our caregivers affect adulthood relationships. It was jointly developed by John Bowlby and Mary Ainsworth in the 1960s. Mary Ainsworth was a graduate of the University of Toronto and specialized in security theory, which emphasizes a child's dependence on their caregiver. Ainsworth, however, sought out a position to work with Bowlby due to his reformulated approach to traditional psychology. Bowlby, a scholar from Cambridge University, was influenced by the professional relationship he had with two young boys upon graduating.

Bowlby became particularly interested in attachment when he began working with teenagers. One of the teenagers he worked with was a withdrawn, indifferent young man who lacked a mother figure. The other was a fearful child who was inseparable from Bowlby. According to *The Origins of Attachment Theory*, the second boy had parents who were either overbearing or entirely absent during his childhood. The stark difference between the two boys and their upbringing is what led Bowlby to begin researching the correlation between upbringing and adult relationships. He wondered: Is there a connection between how a child is treated and how they then go on to treat others? This wonderment, and his subsequent life's work in attempting to answer the question he posed, would be the foundation for attachment theory.

Since the 1960s, attachment theory has gained significant traction and has been supported empirically by doctors and researchers alike. It has been carefully crafted into what it is today, which is a theory that clearly demonstrates how an individual's parenting affects their adult relationships.

Attachment styles, or the way in which different types of childhood experiences emerge in adulthood, come in four basic forms:

1. Dismissive-Avoidant

2. Fearful-Avoidant

3. Anxious Attachment

4. Secure Attachment

Dismissive-Avoidant

Someone with a *Dismissive-Avoidant* attachment style will:

- Generally appear withdrawn

- Be highly independent

- Be emotionally distant in their relationships

- Be less likely to connect on an intimate level

- Find it difficult to be highly involved with their partners

- Become overwhelmed when they are relied on heavily

- Retreat physically and emotionally as a result

Their *core beliefs*, or the recurring perceptions that replay in their subconscious, will perpetuate a sense of defectiveness and uncertainty in relationships. They essentially believe at an innermost level that they are unsafe around people and that vulnerability always results in pain.

Although the Dismissive-Avoidant may appear to have shortcomings in their relationships (as do those with all attachment styles), they can actually be wonderful partners. By having a deeper understanding of why someone is Dismissive-Avoidant, a relationship can be healthier, happier, and more fulfilling.

So, why *is* the Dismissive-Avoidant individual so distant? Adults who are Dismissive-Avoidant typically had parents who were absent from their childhood. This absence can be in the form of physical, emotional, or intellectual abandonment. Since children quite literally depend on their parents for survival, those with neglectful parents have to learn how to self-soothe. Eventually this child is likely to develop a belief that they can only safely rely on themselves. This belief is then subconsciously brought into adulthood and manifests as distant and dismissive behavior. However, this can be remedied over time—a healthy relationship with a Dismissive-Avoidant can be built with consistent emotional support, autonomy, and direct communication.

Fearful-Avoidant

An individual who is *Fearful-Avoidant* will:

- Often demonstrate ongoing ambivalence in relationships—they constantly shift between being vulnerable with their partner and being distant. This behavior is consistent across all their relationships, regardless of whether they are romantic.

- Generally express *depth of processing*—a tendency to overanalyze microexpressions, body language, and language for signs of betrayal. This occurs because they had an untrusting relationship with their caregivers in childhood. Living with a parent who is an addict or emotionally unwell are two examples of what may create this distrust.

- Not trust naturally

- Often feel as if betrayal is always on the horizon

The core wounds for this attachment style revolve around feeling unworthy, being taken advantage of, and feeling unsafe.

Why is the Fearful-Avoidant individual so unpredictable? Their core wounds and tumultuous behavior typically stem from some form of childhood abuse. However, this abuse is paired with one or both parents *also* being emotionally supportive at infrequent times. This combination creates an innate sense of distrust and confusion, and Fearful-Avoidants learn to expect betrayal while also craving love. It also becomes quite difficult for the Fearful-Avoidant to learn a strategy for attaching or bonding to caregivers because of the level of inconsistency.

Moreover, since they perceived love as a chaotic entity from a young age, they tend to have immense internal conflict as adults. They simultaneously want to feel a sense of connection while subconsciously believing it to be a threat. This produces feelings of resentment or frustration that can be later projected onto relationships.

Ultimately, the Fearful-Avoidant shows up in their relationships as a loving partner, and then will become frightened and pull away when they become vulnerable. To be in a successful relationship with a Fearful-Avoidant, the partner or friend must provide a deep connection in a consistent way. This means openness and respect for boundaries, paired with constant reassurance.

Anxious Attachment

Someone with an *Anxious Attachment*:

- Is generally highly self-sacrificing in order to "people-please"

- Fears rejection

- Has a strong fear of being abandoned

Like the Fearful-Avoidant attachment style, the Anxious attachment style results from inconsistency in childhood. However, in the case of the Anxious Attachment, inconsistency is largely derived from absenteeism rather than abuse by or the dysfunction of a caregiver.

Ultimately, what cultivates an Anxious Attachment in a child is the absence of a predictable and consistent caregiver. Their core wounds will include feelings of inadequacy and the expectation of rejection since attention from their parent was continually given, then taken away.

Inconsistent parenting can also be the result of a supportive but often absent parent or other scenarios where a parent has the capacity to attune to their child but not always the availability. Let's use the example of Jonathan. Both of Jonathan's parents work in the military. They are both emotionally available and present with Jonathan throughout his childhood, but they work and travel a lot. One or both of his parents are often away for prolonged periods, and he is left to stay with his grandparents. This inconsistency leaves Jonathan hungry for closeness to his parents. He understands what it means to be close and connected, as his parents have demonstrated this to him. However, the inconsistency becomes very painful for him, and he is always hungry for more closeness when they leave. The inconsistency leaves him hypervigilant and in fear of being abandoned. Since the subconscious mind learns patterns through whatever it is exposed to consistently, it eventually has an entire program around fearing abandonment.

Since one of the only fears that we are biologically born with is the fear of abandonment, erratic parenting constantly triggers anxiety for the child. This fosters a sense of abandonment, and so they sacrifice their needs in adulthood to subconsciously maintain relationships.

The Anxious Attachment will often overcompensate in friendships and romantic relationships to avoid rejection, but this inevitably results in resentment. For the Anxious Attachment, this is because there is often confusion between *compromise* and *sacrifice*. They will often fail to recognize the difference between the two—one being a temporary shift in needs versus the total abandonment of them—and this often breeds conflict long-term. Over time, the Anxious Attachment can often perpetuate unhealthy habits, feel a lack of self-worth, and experience failed relationships.

Although these feelings are triggered from the Anxious Attachment's core wounds, they can be healed. In relationships that are validating, available, and affectionate, the

Anxious Attachment can be an amazing partner and truly grow into themselves.

Secure Attachment

Those with a *Secure attachment* style:

- Are secure in relationships

- Are generally supportive, available, and open with their friends or partners

- Can help shift those of other attachments into a more Secure space and, with the proper tools, can ensure they become Secure altogether.

The Secure Attachment arises from a childhood that has available and supportive parents. They were taught that you can be safe while being vulnerable and that their needs were worthy of being met. In the early studies, children who were secure due to supportive parenting would freely explore when their caregiver was present but would become noticeably upset when they left.

Just as attachment styles are created, they can be transformed. The goal is to move toward a Secure attachment style and away from the aforementioned behaviors. Although other attachment styles do not indicate that someone is inherently flawed, they *can* perpetuate unhealthy habits and reinforce negative beliefs.

By learning about the different attachment styles and how they change in different relationships, you can learn how to heal the dynamic between yourself, your partner, and those closest to you.

You will be equipped to uncover your subconscious mechanisms, and even reprogram your mind. Once you have this knowledge, you can truly begin to better yourself.

A Brief History of Attachment Theory

Now that you better understand each attachment style, more detail can be provided to help you understand how exactly the attachment styles are formed. As mentioned, the Dismissive-Avoidant had a highly neglectful childhood. Typically, they had parents who were completely unavailable in an emotional, physical, or intellectual capacity.

Neglect often begins in early childhood (from birth to three years old). It comes in the form of absenteeism when the infant cries—often, when parents ignore their baby crying, it teaches the child that expressing their emotions is futile and will only be met with rejection. Such rejection during this formative age teaches the child's earliest subconscious programs to expect rejection when expressing their emotions, as noted in the third volume of *Translational Development Psychiatry*. Because the fear of abandonment is one of the only biological fears that humans are born with, the infant will then shift into a low-level state of fight-or-flight.

This mind-set then moves the child into a near-constant existence in their sympathetic nervous system. Physiologically, this means, among other things, that the child has extra cortisol—the stress hormone—being released in their brain. Researchers at Harvard University have called prolonged exposure to cortisol in childhood "toxic" stress. Toxic stress impedes cognitive development, which can produce unsavory behavior in adulthood. Other effects may include impaired brain development, hypersensitivity to stressful situations in adulthood, and long-term emotional dysfunction.

The Dismissive-Avoidant attachment can also be formed in childhood, after the age of three. For example, imagine there is a seven-year-old child named Ross. Ross's parents are physically and emotionally absent from his life. They have high-profile jobs and can afford to send him to private school. However, when he has issues with being bullied at school, they write it off as a typical childhood experience. Since Ross is doing well academically and is still involved in after-school activities, they do not bother to validate his emotions. Consequently, Ross constantly feels alone and comes to subconsciously believe the only person he can rely on to soothe himself *is* himself. As you can see, emotional neglect does not necessarily mean a child was physically abandoned—it can include a wider variety of neglect such as absenteeism or a lack of emotional connection between the caregiver and child.

Moreover, a Dismissive-Avoidant attachment style can also be formed through a combination of emotional neglect from one parent and *enmeshment trauma* from the other. According to Thrivetalk, enmeshment trauma is a form of emotional damage that occurs when one or more parents project their values, needs, and dreams onto their child. This causes the child to abandon their own sense of self in order to please their caregiver. Ultimately, the child feels as though they must adapt to their parent's needs to be worthy of love, and this, when combined with a caregiver who is also unavailable, leaves the child feeling emotionally abandoned.

Eventually, the Dismissive-Avoidant wants to dissociate from those around them because they have an abundance of stored subconscious associations around their emotional vulnerability being rejected. In adulthood, they will sub-consciously feel in control when they are on their own, and will be at peace alone. In their relationships, they will need time alone to soothe themselves because being alone has the most positive childhood associations. Since the sub-conscious is most "comfortable" with what it knows, it will actively work to re-create a sense of familiarity.

For the Dismissive-Avoidant, this means withdrawing in emotionally challenging situations in adulthood. For those who are in a relationship with the Dismissive-Avoidant, or if you are a Dismissive-Avoidant yourself, issues can arise if this coping mechanism is not mutually understood. There-fore, to begin healing yourself or your relationship, you must first understand where these patterns come from, and then learn the steps to finally heal them.

The Fearful-Avoidant has a different history from the Dismissive-Avoidant—they had one or both caregivers who were emotionally volatile or abusive. Parental volatility, in this case, generally comes in the form of addiction, violence, or personality disorders. Despite their unpredictability, the parent could also emotionally connect with their child. This creates a deep-rooted sense of confusion for the child, as the line between nature and nurture becomes blurred. Children are biologically wired to have an attachment to their parents, but when the child *does* connect with their volatile caregiver, it does not feel good.

This volatile connection between parent and child is unpredictable or unsafe, and although the child yearns for closeness, it can be uncomfortable or painful when they attain it. Essentially, they do not form an attachment strat-egy. This is what creates the Fearful-Avoidant's ongoing struggle between being vulnerable in their relationships and being distant. Since, as a child, they do not learn to self-soothe, nor do they feel safe attaching to the caregiver, they are constantly in a state of disorganization. This is why the Fearful-Avoidant is also sometimes referred to as *Anxious-Avoidant* or *Disorganized* in attachment theory. Ultimately, the Fearful-Avoidant begins replaying memories from the past, telling them that deep connection and vulnerability is unsafe—yet they want it so much at the same time.

A Fearful-Avoidant attachment style can also be created by a one-way connection with a parent. This means that one or both parents rely on their child for emotional support, but do not reciprocate. Imagine there is a child named Camila. Camila's parents fight viciously with one another, and her father then constantly turns to her to vent about Camila's mother. To Camila, a child who does not know differently, her emotional needs will feel partially met since there is communication between her and her father. However, she is simultaneously being taught that she is not deserving of receiving the same support that she is providing. It makes her feel like she needs to prove that she is worthy in a relationship and consequently teaches her that to be loved she must self-sacrifice.

Fundamentally, the Fearful-Avoidant attachment style is created by persistent incongruency in parenting. Trust is largely based on consistency, so the Fearful-Avoidant constantly struggles between their natural need for connection and the pain that they've been taught comes with it. Since attachment styles can also be formed in varying magnitudes, it is important to keep in mind that they can be especially strong if trust is broken before the age of eight, when our brains are mainly producing alpha and theta brainwaves—the very same waves that are produced during hypnosis.

If trust between the parent and child is deeply broken as a result of physical, sexual, or emotional abuse, a stronger Fearful attachment style will be created. As with the Dismissive-Avoidant attachment style, the Fearful-Avoidant will essentially play out the patterns that they learned in childhood in order to move into their subconscious comfort zone. This will result in a strong "push-pull" behavior in adulthood relationships where the Fearful-Avoidant will constantly struggle between being connected to their partner or friend and then quickly shifting to being dismissive and withdrawn.

The Anxious attachment style, as mentioned, results more so from absenteeism in childhood than from abuse. The child who grows into an Anxious attachment style has one or more parents who are present and loving one moment, and then absent or unavailable the next. Consequently, they can trust and deeply connect with their parents and then feel a strong emotional hunger when they disappear. As Live Science discusses, connection with caregivers releases oxytocin, among other neurochemicals, in the brain. Immediate withdrawal then creates a more significant sense of longing and a deeper dependency on their parent or parents to be soothed. However, the child will not actually have enough distance to learn how to self-soothe, so they will feel an even deeper need to rely on their caregivers.

Consequently, a subconscious program that revolves around the fear of abandonment begins to be ingrained in the Anxiously attached individual. They will begin to get deeply triggered when the caregiver separates from them and will often feel lonely and unloved because they hunger for closeness. The inconsistency in parental availability for the child ultimately results in the child believing they must self-sacrifice to maintain their caregiver's presence and be worthy of their love. If they do exactly what is demanded of them in relationships, they will subconsciously believe that people will stick around. In adulthood, this eventually creates a strong sense of resentment from the Anxious individual toward those they are sacrificing their needs and values for. Without the understanding of why they are doing this, they will continue to do so and will create turmoil in the relationships they value the most.

Another scenario in which an Anxious attachment style can arise is when one caregiver is incredibly present and connected and the other is very withdrawn—again, a form of inconsistency. This time, imagine there is a child named Parker. He has a father who is ever-present, understanding, and loving. Parker's mother, however, is always busy at work. A constant need to be clingy will arise in him because, while positive associations are being built by his closeness to his father, they are also simultaneously being taken away by his mother. He will eventually try to use *activating strategies*—the process of using past knowledge to make future decisions—to keep his mother from leaving. However, his energy is invested into maintaining closeness to his mother rather than learning how to self-soothe. This is why you'll see the Anxious Attachment in adulthood ultimately working to prevent someone from leaving by doing whatever they perceive that person needs, rather than working on the actual problem at hand.

So, are you, or is someone you love, a Ross, Camila, or Parker? If so, you may now be beginning to understand where these behaviors arise from. This means that you're beginning to have the tools that you need to build a strong, lasting relationship with not only those you love, but with yourself. Ask yourself: *What would you do with the information you have? What would your strategy be for making use of this newfound knowledge?* I would suggest that you write it down and then read the rest of the book and find out if your strategy is correct—or if it will perpetuate old habits.

Let's think of the subconscious mind as a supercomputer. Throughout your life, your subconscious mind stores all memories. You may not necessarily be able to access all of your memories at a conscious level, but the mind stores and consolidates all of your experiences. Within these experiences are your belief patterns, emotional associations, habits, and the concepts you have about the world. These are essentially the programs that shape the way you see your life. They are the filter through which you view your world.

Some of these programs are positive and beneficial, while others can be negative and fear-based. An example of this would be a belief you might carry that says, "Nobody can be trusted." Think of how this belief might impact your relationships with other people.

> *By using your conscious mind to repetitively create new beliefs or behaviors, you can reprogram the patterns in your subconscious mind that cause pain.*

There are many ways to do this. Most involve using repetition of thought or action, combined with emotion. Ultimately, as the Fearful-Avoidant, you must reprogram your subconscious to heal the root causes of the turmoil you experience. This book will give you the tips, tricks, and techniques to do so.

What Is Attachment Theory Used For?

According to the Association for Child and Adolescent Mental Health (ACAMH), attachment theory is widely used by doctors, lawyers, politicians, and teachers alike. Since it helps to describe the relationship between parenting and subsequent development, it is useful in a variety of fields where predicting and understanding behavior is necessary.

Although it is especially helpful when understanding romantic relationships, it can be applied to friendships, familial relationships, and even behavior in the workplace.

Think about it—if you were to truly understand why you behave the way you do, it could, for example, help you get closure with your caregivers who were emotionally neglectful or incongruent in their parenting. Once you understand the pain that you've internalized and how it affects you, you will be able to—with the techniques outlined later in this book—heal yourself and heal any relationships that your attachment style bleeds into.

For example, recall Parker from the previous section. As an adult, he fights with his partner daily because he feels as though he is always the one putting the effort into the relationship. He moved into his partner's apartment in a different city, and he even switched his job to a new industry to do so. His resentment has grown, but he rationalizes his choices, saying that if he didn't do these things the relationship "wouldn't work."

At work, he also feels concerned about his job security when his boss criticizes his projects. Although his boss just wants to move a project in a different direction, Parker takes it personally. With friends, he constantly feels concerned about giving them enough attention amid everything else going on. He is overwhelmed, resentful, and frustrated that he isn't pursuing a career in something he is passionate about.

Now, imagine Parker understood *why* he chose to do, and to worry about, all these things. He has, at his core, an Anxious attachment style. He abandons his needs to, as he perceives, satisfy others to keep them in his life. However, in reality, his growing resentment for his partner is poisoning his relationship. At work, he is unfulfilled because he is in an industry he doesn't enjoy and is taking criticism personally regardless of its intent. With friends, he is unable to show up authentically because of everything else that he has on his plate—and this causes him immense distress because of the programs running in his subconscious.

In each of these cases, Parker need only understand that a healthier version of his life lies in understanding why he makes these choices and their true consequences. By understanding his attachment style, he will be able to *compromise* rather than *sacrifice* in his relationship, will understand the importance of authentically following his career aspirations, and can remove some anxiety from his friendships by understanding that a friend won't just disappear.

Although all this change is easier said than done, this surface-level example sheds some light on how understanding your attachment style truly impacts every area of your life.

Now that you better understand the widespread application of attachment theory, we can also explore the ways in which it also functions across professions such as the medical field, legal field, children's education, and public policy. Not only can attachment theory be applied to different relationships, it can be used to better understand the functionality of various macro-level scenarios. For example, in children's education, understanding attachment theory enables teachers and caretakers to better understand the interactions between students, another example described by the ACAMH. If one student is exhibiting withdrawn behavior, it may be important for the teacher to give the student the space they need to process their emotions before approaching them to discuss the problem. Moreover, applying attachment theory can also potentially indicate if there is aggressive or violent behavior occurring within an adolescent's home, according to research. Furthermore, if the student is continually demonstrating ambivalent behavior, such as aggressive conflict resolution, it may indicate a volatile household. By properly identifying the issue, the teen could be removed and brought to safety. Similar applications of attachment theory can be seen across all professions. Ultimately, attachment theory helps one understand the ways in which people function on an individual level and while interacting with one another.

Although attachment theory has a variety of applications, it tends to be especially useful in couples' therapy. Since each attachment style has generalized trends, understanding your or your partner's coping mechanisms, subconscious beliefs, and perceptions can relieve substantial communication issues. For example, in a relationship, the Dismissive-Avoidant may be withdrawn, autonomous, and seemingly independent. To the Dismissive-Avoidant, they are functioning as they always have—on their own. To an Anxious Attachment, however, it may feel as though their partner is on the verge of abandoning them and may cause serious emotional distress. However, the Dismissive-Avoidant's coping mechanisms don't necessarily mean they are detaching from the *relationship*—they are actually just detaching from *their own emotions*.

Now, although none of these behaviors are necessarily healthy in a relationship, understanding why they occur is the first step. Once partners understand each other's coping mechanisms and vulnerabilities, they can begin to supply their partner with the things that they *do* need. For example, the Dismissive-Avoidant needs continuous and unwavering emotional support and validation. Since they were emotionally neglected as a child, they need to slowly learn that they can consistently and predictably rely on others.

The Anxious Attachment individual needs reassurance and affection to understand that they *are* good enough and that they *won't* be rejected. The simple knowledge of the pain points of your partner and the pain points that lie within yourself opens up a whole stream of communication that you previously were unable to tap into—because your conscious mind didn't even know it was there.

Moreover, your attachment style also interacts with what Dr. Gary Chapman describes as your "Love Language." Just as there are different spoken languages, and different dialects present within the spoken languages, Love Languages are different ways that people express and receive love or gratitude when they interact with others, whether with a romantic partner or with friends and family. According to Dr. Chapman's book, they consist of five different kinds of expressions:

1. Words of affirmation

2. Acts of service

3. Giving and receiving gifts

4. Quality time

5. Physical touch

Given the attachment style of each partner in a relationship, certain expressions may be better received. Attachment theory applies to a variety of circumstances and works well paired with other theories to make couples therapy a more holistic experience. The following chapters will dive into what your attachment style is, what it means, and how it functions in all aspects of your life—from your romantic relationships to your friendships with coworkers.

Chapter 2

HOW ATTACHMENT THEORY APPLIES TO YOU

Chapter 2 examines two important concepts: how attachment styles are fluid and how to discover your attachment style. You will come to learn that your attachment style can vary among *types* of relationships, such as friendships, romantic relationships, or familial relationships. For example, if one friend begins to perpetuate a toxic relationship, it does not necessarily mean that the subconscious beliefs created will be brought into romantic relationships.

This chapter will also explore how subconscious beliefs in one area of one kind of relationship—such as within one specific friendship—can then spread to other friendships and create challenges.

By understanding how your attachment style can flex and be shaped, you will be able to better understand what kind of attachment you have in different areas of your life. Once you understand this concept in more detail, you can take a quiz to truly find out where your attachments lie. In the following chapters, you will be taught how to move your attachment style toward a more secure attachment.

Find Your Attachment Style

As the subconscious processes more information, core beliefs can be rewritten, and attachments will consequently shift.

Traditionally, attachment styles have been viewed and applied to individuals as static characterizations. In other words, when someone knows they are Dismissive-Avoidant, they often believe they are solely that attachment style. However, this is a surface-level explanation. It acknowledges their primary attachment style, but people are actually composed of each attachment type in different proportions. If a child had parents who were both abusive and emotionally negligent, they may express a stronger combination of Dismissive-Avoidant and Fearful-Avoidant characteristics, with the latter likely being more dominant. They would then have a lower proportion of Secure Attachment and Anxious Attachment tendencies. This is because attachment styles exist along a spectrum.

This is why an individual's attachment style can flex in different relationships—someone could be on the more anxious side of Fearful-Avoidant, for example, depending on the quantity and significance of the experiences they have had. Supporting this claim, a recent study released from the University of Ottawa examined the relationships of 2,214 individuals. It revealed that someone may have a substantially different attachment with their parents, for example, than they do with a partner with a Secure attachment style. Again, this reinforces the idea of attachment styles existing along a sliding spectrum. As individuals encounter new events and relationships that reinforce or disprove their subconscious beliefs, their attachment can shift over time.

This brings up the most important question for healing your attachment style: *What is an attachment trauma?*

Begin by recalling that your attachment style is essentially a set of beliefs about human interaction that is ingrained in your subconscious mind. Since your subconscious is programmed through the combination of repetition and emotion, your attachment style is created through repetitive events that induce strong feelings such as fear or loneliness.

> ### *Your subconscious essentially comes to believe what it perceives it is told over time.*

To illustrate this concept, imagine there is a girl named Sophie. She experienced physical abuse as a child and has come to feel unsafe and uncomfortable while being vulnerable in her romantic relationships. However, Sophie's partner, Riley, has a Secure Attachment because she was raised by supportive parents. Consequently, Riley continuously supports Sophie and validates her emotions. This makes Sophie feel worthy of love and safe in the relationship. Over time, Sophie's subconscious belief that vulnerability is unsafe begins to be reprogrammed because Riley has shown her through a combination of repetition plus emotion that her childhood subconscious beliefs are outdated. This is how one begins to shift into a different form of attachment in a specific relationship. However, Sophie could still be subject to abuse when she sees her parents, which is what perpetuates her Fearful-Avoidant side in her parental relationship.

This occurrence can be seen across all attachment styles and can even be reversed for the Secure partner. Imagine that Riley has a good relationship with Sophie, but that she also has a close friend who begins to treat Riley poorly. The friend constantly overwhelms Riley with information about her life but does not take the time to listen to what is going on in Riley's life. The friend even goes so far as to criticize Riley when Riley attempts to confide in her. Slowly, Riley's subconscious begins to believe that she is unworthy of receiving the love that she gives. Then, in *all* of her friendships, she begins to develop a Fearful-Avoidant attachment. She becomes uncomfortable with vulnerability and begins to self-sacrifice more frequently. Without recognizing these subconscious patterns, Riley will continue to put herself through emotional turmoil and will begin to self-sacrifice to please friends as her subconscious beliefs get perpetuated.

To better understand how attachment style in one relationship type can go on to negatively affect other relationships of the same type, the University of Kansas conducted a study that evaluated two aspects of platonic attachment styles:

1. Tie strength: how close the ties are in an individual's network.

2. Multiplexity: how many roles are filled by the individuals in the network.

This study noted that those who had high Avoidant tendencies had weaker tie strength *and* multiplexity. However, those who were Anxious were significantly less likely to dissolve the ties, but friends would often feel smothered and make moves to dissolve the relationship themselves.

The University of Kansas study demonstrates the latter of a two-part proposition:

1. That attachment styles can vary based on type—for example, friendship or a romantic relationship.

2. That how a person behaves in one relationship—for example, with one specific friend—can spread to how they behave in other relationships of that same type—such as with other friends. This concept is important because it truly demonstrates the ability of the subconscious to store and replay beliefs based on repetition and emotion.

Now that you understand the fluidity of attachment styles and why they lie along a spectrum, you can begin to discover your dominant attachment style in different areas of your life. Consider how you act and feel in your relationships, whether they are romantic, platonic, or familial. Examine the ratio of *activating* to *deactivating* strategies in your thoughts and behaviors. Recall that activating strategies are decisions that are made based on prior information and experiences. Deactivating strategies are actions that drive self-reliance and deny attachment needs altogether, pushing others away. If you have relatively more activating strategies, you may have a greater fear of abandonment and be on the Anxious side of the spectrum. More deactivating strategies may indicate a subconscious belief around complete autonomy, placing you more on the Dismissive-Avoidant side of the attachment scale.

Keep in mind that this tool should be used in romantic relationships after the honeymoon phase is over, a phase that occurs during the first two years of the relationship. During the honeymoon phase, your brain has higher levels of dopamine in the caudate nucleus and ventral tegmental regions, according to *Scientific American*. These areas of the brain are responsible for, respectively, learning and memory and emotional processing. Consequently, your attachment style may be unclear to you in the early phases of your romantic relationship since your emotions, memory, and hormone regulation are atypical.

Our experiences can also dramatically alter our attachment style. For example, if Sophie were to partake in certain forms of therapy and practices such as recurrent meditation, she may be able to better understand and re-equilibrate her subconscious beliefs. According to *Science Daily*, since meditation induces theta brain waves and activates areas of the frontal lobe associated with emotional regulation, Sophie could eventually bring herself into a more Secure attachment space without the help of a Secure partner.

However, although it is common to express different attachment styles in different areas of life, the type of attachment you have in relationships ultimately tends to be the attachment style that you associate with the *type* of relationship. For example, you can be Dismissive-Avoidant in familial relationships because you experienced emotional neglect from parental figures, but you could also be Fearful-Avoidant in romantic relationships due to domestic abuse that has occurred. This illustrates that major events such as betrayal, loss, or abuse can alter our attachment style in different chapters of life, but that ultimately attachment styles are fluid and often dependent on the kind of relationships we are in.

We tend to have a primary attachment style, most associated with how we show up in romantic relationships, that plays a large role in our personality structure. This essentially dictates how we give and receive love and what our subconscious expectations are of others.

Now that you have the background on what attachment styles are, how they are formed, and in what ways they can be shaped and shifted, take the test below. Here you will learn your primary attachment style and—eventually—how you can move toward a Secure style of attachment.

Attachment Theory Quiz

Directions: This quiz is designed to determine your attachment style. In the statements below, circle the answers that sound most like yourself. Refer to the key to find your primary attachment style, along with other attachment-style tendencies that exist within you.

1. I can be very emotionally present with others, but it takes me a while to share vulnerable things about myself.
2. I practice excellent self-care for both myself and my partner.
3. I often put my partner on a pedestal.
4. I easily feel irritated or impatient around my partner.
5. I feel comfortable around my partner and enjoy their company.
6. I have a strong desire for deep conversation in a romantic relationship.
7. I feel very upset when others infringe on my need for space or time alone.
8. I prefer not to spend much time alone.
9. I do not make whimsical decisions about leaving a relationship.
10. I tend to quite frequently be out of touch with my emotions.
11. I am very attuned to my partner's needs and notice when there is any change in behavior.
12. I express my emotions easily.
13. I constantly want to be emotionally closer to my partner.

14. I know how to process my emotions effectively when I feel upset.
15. I easily notice a change in people's microexpressions, body language, and tone of voice.
16. I worry that my partner will fall out of love with me or eventually get bored of me.
17. I am effective at compromising and communicating.
18. I have very strong emotions in relationships.
19. I strongly dislike feeling vulnerable to others.
20. If I notice my partner showing any signs of coldness, I panic and want to get closer as quickly as possible.
21. I do not hold grudges easily or keep resentments long.
22. I often express anger very strongly when I feel hurt, powerless, or betrayed.
23. I don't feel as if boundaries are necessary between myself and a romantic partner.
24. I feel as though conflict is resolvable and feel equipped to work through problems effectively.
25. It is not uncommon for me to experience inward emotional turbulence throughout the duration of a romantic relationship.
26. I can be cold and standoffish at times when I don't know others very well.
27. I often feel very hot or very cold toward my partner or loved one.
28. I know that I am worthy of a healthy, happy relationship.
29. I usually wish that my partner would take care of their own emotions and needs and involve me less.
30. When I feel hurt, I often have thoughts about leaving the relationship immediately.
31. I do not feel as though I need anything from my romantic partner.

32. I am good at listening to other people's needs and expressing my own.
33. I often worry that my partner will reject me or pull away.
34. I do not enjoy being out of relationships.
35. If my partner's behavior hurts me, I will express my feelings and try to understand what caused them to act that way.
36. Relationships are often confusing or emotionally difficult for me.
37. I do not like making social plans with others in advance.
38. I sometimes feel as though I am constantly chasing my partner's love and affection.
39. I find it difficult to trust others in a romantic relationship and am often suspicious.
40. I find that setting boundaries comes naturally to me.
41. There have been times when I have threatened to leave the relationship and then changed my mind.
42. I often avoid conflict and feel very hurt by criticism.
43. I am not afraid of commitment, but I do not jump into relationships without assessing them first.
44. I am afraid that if I ask too much from my partner they will leave me.
45. I focus much more on the relationships in my life than I do on myself.
46. I develop feelings easily but feel as if I'm constantly doubting or questioning them as I get closer to my partner.
47. Sometimes the idea of commitment in a romantic relationship makes me feel afraid or invaded.
48. I often feel protective over my space, privacy, and belongings.

49. I am emotionally stable in my romantic relationships.
50. I tend to operate in extremes between being very emotionally available and then requiring time and space to myself.
51. I find it too easy to open up to people and sometimes overshare with others.
52. I do not express my emotions to others easily.
53. I don't tend to overshare, but I do not fear sharing my feelings with a partner.
54. I generally feel invaded when my partner demands too much physical affection.
55. I hunger for closeness, but often fear being truly vulnerable to my partner.
56. I find it much easier to process my emotions on my own than with others.
57. I would prefer to spend most of my free time with my partner.
58. I feel that it is easy to express my needs to my romantic partner.
59. I find that my partner usually emotionally recovers from conflict before I do.
60. I deeply fear being abandoned by my partner.

KEY

FA = Fearful-Avoidant
DA = Dismissive-Avoidant
S = Secure
A = Anxious

1) FA	21) S	41) FA
2) S	22) FA	42) DA
3) A	23) A	43) S
4) DA	24) S	44) A
5) S	25) FA	45) A
6) FA	26) DA	46) FA
7) DA	27) FA	47) DA
8) A	28) S	48) DA
9) S	29) DA	49) S
10) DA	30) FA	50) FA
11) FA	31) DA	51) A
12) A	32) S	52) DA
13) A	33) A	53) S
14) S	34) A	54) DA
15) FA	35) S	55) FA
16) A	36) FA	56) DA
17) S	37) DA	57) A
18) FA	38) A	58) S
19) DA	39) FA	59) DA
20) A	40) S	60) A

Add up your results in each category using the key above. Remember, we are not a single attachment style. Your answers will provide you with your primary attachment style, along with the tendencies you share with other attachment styles.

Fearful-Avoidant (FA): _____

Dismissive-Avoidant (DA): _____

Secure (S): _____

Anxious (A): _____

Once you've determined your results from the quiz above, it is recommended that you take a closer look at the initial core wounds and attachment patterns explained in chapter 1. In the following pages, the next quiz will allow you to determine the attachment style of your partner or loved one. You can apply the results of both quizzes to the latter part of this chapter, where you will learn about the patterned interactions between different attachment styles.

As you come to more deeply understand the interactions between your attachment style and the styles of your loved ones, you will be empowered to communicate more effectively. You will also be able to understand what your sensitivities are in relationships and what is likely to trigger your loved ones. You'll then be provided with tools and strategies that will allow you to break through the limitations that might exist as a result of conflicting attachment dynamics.

It is important to remember that your attachment style results are not a diagnosis. These are simply a set of patterns that you've developed over time as a result of your experiences. These patterns can be changed with intention, or they may change as a result of exposure to new experiences. Through awareness of these patterns of relating to others, you have a greater chance to thrive in your relationships.

How to Find a Friend's or Partner's Attachment Style

Once you've determined the results from the following quiz, you can go back and review the core wounds and needs from chapter 1 to better understand your loved one. While this isn't a way to diagnose your loved one, it is a way to think about what life is like from their perspective.

This will help prevent you from personalizing their actions and behaviors as often. It will also help you communicate in a way that makes it more likely for you to be heard and will assist you in more effectively moving through conflicts to a space of resolution. The more insight we can bring to our relationships, the easier it becomes to create healthy patterns and thrive in our connection.

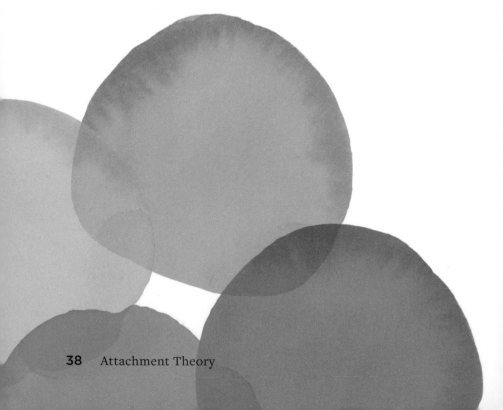

Relationship and Friendship Quiz

Think of the friend, partner, or loved one whose attachment style you are trying to determine. Answer the following questions with this very person in mind. Choose the answer that best describes the individual.

1. When asked to commit to planning in advance, this individual:
   a. Avoids making a commitment as much as possible
   b. Makes commitments but frequently cancels or alters them later
   c. Jumps at the opportunity and goes out of their way to meet
   d. Assesses their schedule and is enthusiastic about meeting if or when available

2. When a conflict arises, this person:
   a. Avoids conflict as much as possible and withdraws
   b. Easily expresses their feelings and needs and listens well to others
   c. Can become emotionally volatile and sometimes angry
   d. May get emotional and tries desperately to repair the relationship

3. The day after this person expresses more vulnerability than usual, they:
   a. Withdraw significantly for days at a time
   b. Feel closer to you but without expectation
   c. Become clingy or expectant

d. Withdraw a little bit but come back
around quickly

4. After an argument or disagreement takes place in
the relationship, this individual:

   a. Feels very guilty, anxious, and tries to
   create more closeness very quickly
   b. Withdraws easily
   c. Expresses understanding and forgiveness
   d. Will sometimes try to get close and at
   other times withdraws noticeably

5. When you express vulnerability or deep emotion,
this person:

   a. Can remain present with you and listen
   b. Will be very present and take on the
   problem as if it's their own but will often
   withdraw later
   c. Will try to bond with you over the vulnerability as much as possible
   d. Sometimes acts cold and creates space

6. When you are at a social event with other people,
this person:

   a. Clings to you and stays by your side
   b. Oscillates between being very close and
   disappearing suddenly
   c. Works to maintain their independence
   and space
   d. Makes you feel comfortable and relaxed

7. When it comes to expressing love or affection,
this individual:

     a. Expresses often and easily

     b. Is very slow to express love and affection and does so sparingly

     c. Expresses a lot of love, but can also express of a lot of negative emotion

     d. Expresses consistently and frequently

8. This individual expresses their needs:

     a. Calmly and easily

     b. Rarely, though they express their emotions all the time

     c. Easily when they are irritated, though they do not express their emotions

     d. In a volatile way that seems to come out of nowhere sometimes

9. When this individual is going through personal challenges, they:

     a. Reach out to others to get soothing and avoid being alone

     b. Withdraw completely from the world

     c. Oscillate between expressing emotions intensely and withdrawing

     d. Spend time processing their thoughts alone, but also lean on others easily

10. When this individual discusses marriage or children, they:

     a. Express optimism and enthusiasm

     b. Deflect or withdraw in the conversation

     c. Express importance and urgency

     d. Often make negative comments about commitment or trust

11. This person fears rejection or abandonment:

a. All the time
b. After a fight
c. Rarely at all
d. If they do feel afraid, they will share it and work through it

12. When this individual is offended, they:

    a. Become passive-aggressive
    b. Lash out
    c. Become sad and worried
    d. Express their feelings and needs

13. If this person's romantic partner were to be hit on by another person, this person would likely:

    a. Get very angry and pull away
    b. Simply pull away and withdraw
    c. Express a boundary and need
    d. Become very anxious and try to get as close to their partner as possible

14. If I needed to depend on this person, I would likely see them:

    a. Show up excessively to help, even to the point of self-sacrifice
    b. Show up excessively to help, but then resent me for it
    c. Withdraw and fear being depended on
    d. Be very supportive, but within the boundaries that work for them

15. If I were to pull back or become cold, this individual would:

    a. Withdraw as well
    b. Become very worried and try to get closer to me immediately
    c. Inquire suspiciously
    d. Try to understand me and express how it affects them

16. When I see this person after being apart for a while, they:

    a. Act a bit standoffish or withdrawn at the beginning
    b. Express warmth immediately, sometimes to the point of being overwhelming
    c. Will sometimes be very warm, and at other times standoffish
    d. Be comfortable, warm, and excited to see me

17. This person makes me feel:

    a. Seen, heard, and understood
    b. Disconnected at times
    c. Confused sometimes, with their swings between hot and cold
    d. Worshipped and adored but sometimes smothered

18. If I were to act out in the relationship, my partner or friend would likely:

    a. Forgive me, but still show up and have their own boundaries as well

    b. Try very hard to fix everything and look for reassurance

    c. Respond spitefully, then express guilt for their actions

    d. Withdraw very strongly, sometimes for days at a time

KEY

1) a = DA, b = FA, c = A, d = S
2) a = DA, b = S, c = FA, d = A
3) a = DA, b = S, c = A, d = FA
4) a = A, b = DA, c = S, d = FA
5) a = S, b = FA, c = A, d = DA
6) a = A, b = FA, c = DA, d = S
7) a = A, b = DA, c = FA, d = S
8) a = S, b = A, c = DA, d = FA
9) a = A, b = DA, c = FA, d = S
10) a = S, b = DA, c = A, d = FA
11) a = A, b = FA, c = DA, d = S
12) a = DA, b = FA, c = A, d = S
13) a = FA, b = DA, c = S, d = A
14) a = A, b = FA, c = DA, d = S
15) a = DA, b = A, c = FA, d = S
16) a = DA, b = A, c = FA, d = S
17) a = S, b = DA, c = FA, d = A
18) a = S, b = A, c = FA, d = DA

Fearful-Avoidant (FA): _____

Dismissive-Avoidant (DA): _____

Secure (S): _____

Anxious (A): _____

Using the answers above, tally the number of times that each style (FA, DA, S, and A) appears within the responses. Determine their primary attachment style (the one occurring most often), and then refer to the following section to learn more about interactions between different attachment styles and the patterns you can become aware of in order to best support and enrich the relationship.

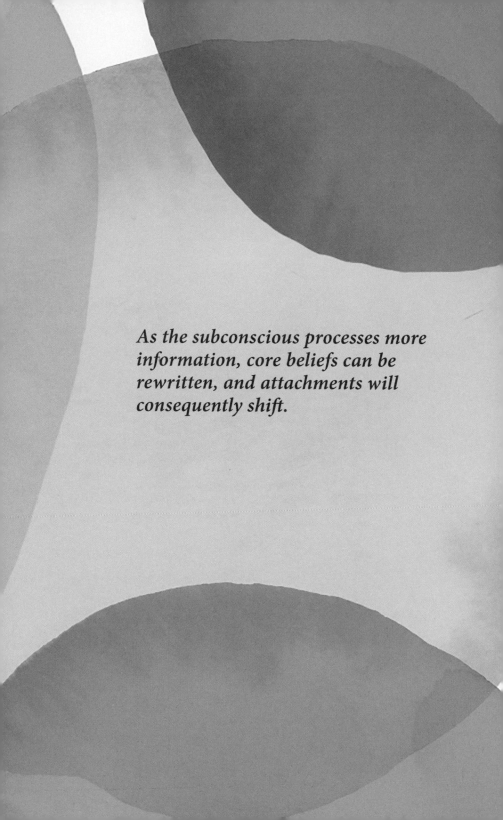

As the subconscious processes more information, core beliefs can be rewritten, and attachments will consequently shift.

Part 2

THE BASIC FOUR[2]

Since we have examined the traits and behaviors of the four main attachment styles, we can now delve into how these attachments relate to one another. It is important to remember that attachment styles exist along a spectrum. Most people have a dominant attachment style, but they can also have varying degrees or combinations of other attachment styles. Learning to navigate your attachment style will help you understand your strengths and vulnerabilities in a relationship. We will discuss the highs and lows and the positive and negative factors that affect each combination of attachment styles.

This next section will act as a basic guide to various combinations that two people, or "partners," fall into. The term *partner* can be used for two people who are involved romantically or to describe relationships between friends or family members.

As mentioned earlier, different attachment styles essentially play the game of connection by using a different set of rules. Different needs, desires, and expectations about what a relationship should look like can create many difficulties within a relationship.

Understanding what patterns and beliefs you bring into a relationship will enable you to navigate and make stronger connections with others, creating a healthy and empowering relationship. Being aware and using the tools provided by this book will enable you to transform your limitations in your relationships with others, allowing for a deeper connection. Awareness is the first step to transformation, and you will learn how to heal yourself and your partner, allowing for a more satisfying and connected relationship.

SECURE & SECURE ATTACHMENT STYLE

If life were perfect, all relationships would include two Securely attached partners. Two Secure partners will generally experience ease in expressing their feelings and needs to one another. As mentioned in chapter 1, the securely attached individual had caregivers that were good at meeting their needs consistently. As a result, this individual was conditioned to feel that their needs were worthy of being met and that the expression of emotion was healthy.

If a relationship is open, honest, and equal, both people feel independent and can readily "give and take" when need be. They turn to their partner when they need to and feel supported. There is also a healthy capacity to compromise and to express vulnerability. For example, one partner may say, "I know you are stressed and feeling overwhelmed today, but I would really appreciate if you could be more present with me when you have the opportunity." Validation is given for what the person is feeling emotionally.

Conflict is a necessary part of human interaction. It is how we break down invisible walls and perceived imbalances in a relationship. Conflict often creates deeper bonds between two individuals when effectively resolved, and it can still take place between two securely attached individuals.

Two Securely attached partners are more likely to feel safe expressing their feelings and needs to one another. They are also less likely to have negatively stored associations with conflict that arise from childhood experiences. Thus, they are more effective in communicating and maintaining mutual respect and trust while in conflict. There is no right or wrong when arguing, but effective communication allows them to maintain respect and express vulnerabilities.

The lows that an individual may experience in this attachment dynamic tend to be significantly less than in relationships with insecure attachment bonds.

SECURE & DISMISSIVE-AVOIDANT ATTACHMENT STYLE

The Secure person tends to work very well with their Dismissive-Avoidant partner. Secure partners will sometimes feel like their Dismissive-Avoidant counterpart is mysterious or confusing. Since the Dismissive-Avoidant is highly independent, a Secure partner may want more closeness or commitment in the relationship. They will express this in a straightforward and direct way, usually without criticism so that the Dismissive-Avoidant doesn't feel like their partner is becoming too clingy or needy. This relationship often creates a platform where both partners become more Secure over time.

The highs are that the Secure partner often feels very grateful because the Dismissive-Avoidant is often non-committal and fearful of too much emotion. The Secure values the Dismissive-Avoidant partner and will nurture them in a way that the Dismissive-Avoidant didn't receive in relationships growing up.

The lows are that the Secure partner can become impatient with their Dismissive-Avoidant's difficulty in making a commitment, and they might feel stonewalled during communication. The fact that the Dismissive-Avoidant doesn't open up easily or share enough can be very frustrating for the Secure partner. This could make the Secure partner want to leave the relationship as they need more than they are getting.

SECURE & FEARFUL-AVOIDANT ATTACHMENT STYLE

The attachment dynamic between a Secure and a Fearful-Avoidant individual tends to be slightly more challenging than between two Secure partners.

The Fearful-Avoidant is often a very present and charming partner in the early stages of a relationship. They are dialed into human behavior and know what their partner is looking for. It is not uncommon for the Fearful-Avoidant to morph into what they believe their partner wants as a strategy to feel accepted and worthy of love. As discussed in chapter 1, it is quite common for a Fearful-Avoidant to have grown up in a home where they experienced significant distress. To adapt, this individual is a keen observer and becomes hypervigilant, especially about human behavior. They will quickly and without trying notice microexpressions, body language, and changes in intonation. The Fearful-Avoidant learns this hyperawareness to protect themselves from potential conflict.

The highs are that a Secure and Fearful-Avoidant can share a great capacity for seeing, hearing, and understanding one another. They have a need for deep conversation and discussing their fears, concerns, and secrets.

The lows for the Secure partner are that when a Fearful-Avoidant begins to develop stronger feelings, they will tend to push their partner away. They believe that this relationship is too good to be true and don't trust such a stable and safe partnership.

In a friendship or family relationship, the same patterns are maintained. However, the Fearful-Avoidant will usually be less emotionally volatile and less vulnerable at the root level. The fear of powerlessness is not as strong, and therefore the Fearful-Avoidant experiences less of a roller coaster in their nonromantic relationships.

SECURE & ANXIOUS ATTACHMENT STYLE

While the Secure and Anxious relationship can have its challenges, this duo often works well together after the initial pain points are worked through.

The Anxious partner can be very needy and insecure at first. They put themselves down and put their partner on a pedestal. The Secure partner is available to give the positive reinforcement and validation that the anxious partner craves. Over time, with emotional stability and reprogramming, many of the Anxious individual's patterns will change to feelings of stability, and they will require less attention and support from the Secure partner.

The highs for the Secure are that they feel loved and adored by their Anxious partner because their needs are met, and they spend a significant amount of time together. There is a consistency and stability as each partner learns what to expect from the other over time.

The lows for the Secure partner are that when the Anxious acts desperate or insecure, their behavior exacerbates their own fears and they become demanding and possessive toward their partner. The Secure partner may feel like they need to take a step back and regain their space to keep their sense of self.

DISMISSIVE-AVOIDANT & SECURE ATTACHMENT STYLE

The initial fear of commitment expressed by the Dismissive-Avoidant tends to work very well with the Secure attachment partner. The Secure partner is able to extend the security, predictability, and consistency that the Dismissive-Avoidant finds so appealing. The aloof, cold Dismissive-Avoidant responds to the safety that the Secure loved one can offer.

The Dismissive-Avoidant is usually afraid of feeling too much emotion and tends to cut themselves off from their partner as emotional closeness ensues. The Secure partner offers direct communication and encouragement and respects their need for space and autonomy.

The highs for the Dismissive-Avoidant are that they come to believe that they can open up and trust with a Secure partner who will ultimately bring out the best in them, nurturing them and thereby giving them what they didn't receive in childhood.

The lows for the Dismissive-Avoidant revolve around their subconscious programs of feeling unsafe and vulnerable around people. They may be unable to open up or share enough with their partner and therefore unable to commit to a serious relationship.

DISMISSIVE-AVOIDANT & DISMISSIVE-AVOIDANT ATTACHMENT STYLE

This is a relationship of two counterparts who emotionally distance themselves from one another. They seek isolation and they are focused on themselves. This is an attachment-style relationship that may be short-lived due to each partner being emotionally unavailable.

Since both partners share the same attachment style of being introverted and detaching themselves from each other, feelings are not communicated easily, and bonding is difficult. This relationship will probably not become serious as both partners are highly independent and unwilling to be vulnerable in a meaningful way.

The highs are that the Dismissive-Avoidant won't have to worry about a clingy or needy partner. Both will rely on themselves and not feel pressure to provide emotional commitment in the relationship. There is less conflict and less involvement.

The lows are that the Dismissive-Avoidants may find it difficult to commit or connect deeply. Due to the lack of sharing, the Dismissive-Avoidants may simply walk away before the relationship becomes too involved.

In other relationships, Dismissive-Avoidants will be less likely to connect with friends, and they will be less involved in conflict with their familial ties.

DISMISSIVE-AVOIDANT & **FEARFUL-AVOIDANT** ATTACHMENT STYLE

This relationship combination can work in some ways, as both partners have many similarities and can have similar coping mechanisms. The Fearful-Avoidant appears warm, is hypersensitive to what others think, and is readily available to please the Dismissive-Avoidant.

The Fearful-Avoidant is generally very loving and giving, and the Dismissive-Avoidant can warm up to this connection. However, the Dismissive-Avoidant can be aloof and not want as much closeness as their partner.

Even though both styles of attachment cause each partner to derive security from their own individual space, the Fearful-Avoidant's anxious side is usually triggered by their Dismissive-Avoidant partner, and they will therefore become more anxious and reliant on their partner. The Dismissive-Avoidant will not feel guilt or remorse if space is taken; however, the Fearful-Avoidant may shut down and feel neglected when the Dismissive-Avoidant pulls away.

The highs for the Dismissive-Avoidant in this dynamic are that they feel deeply seen, heard, understood, and valued by their Fearful-Avoidant partner. The Dismissive-Avoidant also appreciates that the Fearful-Avoidant needs their space.

The lows for the Dismissive-Avoidant in this dynamic are when their Fearful-Avoidant partner becomes emotionally volatile or critical. This can trigger a core wound that arose from feeling emotionally unsafe in childhood and lead them to further assume abandonment will take place.

DISMISSIVE-AVOIDANT
& ANXIOUS
ATTACHMENT STYLE

This relationship dynamic can be challenging without the proper tools. The difficulty arises when the Dismissive-Avoidant seeks out a partner that appreciates their need for independence. Meanwhile, the Anxious Attachment will go out of their way to create emotional closeness, and this may scare off the Dismissive-Avoidant.

The inconsistency of their early caregiver's presence triggered ongoing anxiety in the Anxious Attachment. As a result, the Anxious partner will overcompensate in a relationship because they are afraid of rejection. They will continually "give" to the Dismissive-Avoidant partner, sacrificing their own needs and then feeling disappointed or confused when their partner doesn't act the same way. When the Dismissive-Avoidant pulls away, this creates extreme anxiety and exposes the relationship to turmoil and pain.

The highs for the Dismissive-Avoidant in this relationship come from how worshipped and supported they feel. The inexhaustible love seemingly displayed by the Anxious partner allows the Dismissive-Avoidant partner to feel safe.

The lows for the Dismissive-Avoidant are when they experience the roller coaster of emotions from their partner. The tendency for the Anxious to cling often makes the Dismissive-Avoidant feel invaded, trapped, and flustered. They then withdraw, causing more activating strategies for the Anxious. In this relationship, not using proper strategies for communication often leads to a vicious cycle.

ANXIOUS & FEARFUL-AVOIDANT ATTACHMENT STYLE

An Anxious Attachment would likely feel more comfortable with a Fearful-Avoidant at first. The ability for both attachment styles to attune and connect with one another can feel like fireworks. The Anxious will often feel like they have met their match! Both partners connect deeply and easily at the beginning of the relationship.

However, when the Fearful-Avoidant experiences vulnerability, they begin feeling triggered, and this can create unexpected changes. As the feelings get stronger and the fearful partner withdraws, it is very painful for the Anxious. This reintroduces the mixed signals that their parents gave them in childhood and continues to perpetuate the Anxious individual's belief that they are unworthy or unlovable.

The highs for the Anxious individual include the strong emotional connection that occurs. The Anxious Attachment often feels the Fearful-Avoidant's presence and passion and experiences profound infatuation.

The low point for the Anxious is the immense anxiety that is created when the Fearful-Avoidant withdraws. Because of the extreme polarities the Fearful-Avoidant can bring to the table, the Anxious may be feel completely overwhelmed and rejected.

ANXIOUS & ANXIOUS ATTACHMENT STYLE

Two Anxious Attachments in a relationship ultimately creates more anxiety, regardless of the relationship's type. Although it may be intuitive to believe that two of the same attachment styles could find fulfillment together, their relationship usually just perpetuates the negative subconscious beliefs that they already have.

A high of the relationship is the emotional connection that occurs as both anxious individuals look desperately for closeness. This hunger for closeness will often create a pattern of simultaneous self-sacrifice.

The low points are likely to set in unless these partners develop healthy strategies for connection. Both Anxious Attachments are likely to keep giving what they perceive the other values, and this will ultimately create significant resentment in the relationship. This is especially prevalent when neither partner is very comfortable at truly expressing their needs. These are the breeding grounds for expectation and miscommunication.

ANXIOUS & SECURE ATTACHMENT STYLE

Someone with an Anxious attachment style is very likely to self-sabotage in relationships of all kinds due to the fear of abandonment that they have as a core wound. Since they experienced inconsistency in childhood through both parental presence and absence, they subconsciously fear that their partner will abandon them. This produces strong feelings of unworthiness, loneliness, and anxiety in the Anxious individual.

Their dynamic with a Secure Attachment tends to be very positive because it inevitably teaches their subconscious more positive beliefs. Unfortunately, Anxious Attachments are typically unlikely to seek out a Secure partner because this attachment style is unfamiliar to their subconscious. Recall that the subconscious always attempts to re-create what it "knows."

However, the Secure Attachment, which tends to be consistent, reassuring, and open to communication, provides the Anxious Attachment with the connection that they are so hungry for. However, this won't stop the Anxious Attachment from continuing to overcompensate and people please out of a fear of abandonment. The Anxious Attachment must work on healing those core wounds themselves. However, with a Secure Attachment, there will be more space for them to heal those wounds while still feeling connected and validated by the Secure Attachment.

One of the highs experienced by the Anxious Attachment is the loving bond they will receive from their Secure partner. The Secure is also very patient, understanding, and reassuring. This can help the Anxious Attachment partner to settle into a healthy relationship over time.

The lows that can exist often spring from when the Anxious individual continues to self-sacrifice. This will produce a sense of resentment in the relationship as they slowly erode their values to please the Secure individual. Therefore, the Anxious Attachment must continue to work on expressing their needs and boundaries.

ANXIOUS & DISMISSIVE-AVOIDANT ATTACHMENT STYLE

The Anxious Attachment and Dismissive-Avoidant relationship can be a tricky one. The Dismissive-Avoidant will pull away when they feel overwhelmed by emotional connection. For the Anxious Attachment, this becomes very painful and reinforces existing beliefs of inevitable rejection and unworthiness.

Regardless of whether the relationship is romantic, platonic, or familial, the Anxious Attachment will continue to sacrifice their needs to get closer to the Dismissive-Avoidant. This will cause internal conflict in the Anxious Attachment because their subconscious will continuously be told to forgo emotional connection when that is what they thirst for the most.

Eventually, the Anxious Attachment can even come to play "games" with their partner to attempt to quell the insecurity they feel with their partner. Sometimes, this includes threatening to leave the relationship for the momentary connection they feel with their Dismissive-Avoidant partner who might express vulnerability in those rare moments. This creates a highly unhealthy dynamic in the relationship that will continue to be perpetuated until both individuals recognize their core wounds.

Ultimately, the Dismissive-Avoidant needs a partner who provides them with constant reassurance. If the Dismissive-Avoidant were to work on being connected with the Anxious Attachment, they would find that the Anxious Attachment provides them with the predictable affection and validation that they need. This would be a best-case scenario in this relationship.

As mentioned, the Anxious partner may also threaten to leave the relationship out of desperation. This sort of manipulative tactic would represent a relationship low, as it reinforces negative beliefs that both attachment styles have about themselves.

FEARFUL-AVOIDANT & DISMISSIVE-AVOIDANT ATTACHMENT STYLE

The Fearful-Avoidant and Dismissive-Avoidant will likely have a difficult relationship. The Dismissive-Avoidant will not provide the intense, emotional fulfillment that the Fearful-Avoidant looks for.

This can lead to the Fearful-Avoidant feeling rejected and withdrawing over time, creating more distance in the relationship. Moreover, the Dismissive-Avoidant will likely feel overwhelmed by the Fearful-Avoidant's strong presence. This could result in frustration for both parties and emotional chaos in the relationship.

However, the Dismissive-Avoidant will not respond to the Fearful-Avoidant with an outburst of emotion—something that would be especially triggering to the Fearful-Avoidant. In a sense, this would introduce stability into the relationship, to which the Fearful-Avoidant is unaccustomed. This would be a high of the relationship—an absence of a feeling of "unsafe" for the Fearful-Avoidant.

However, the low is the lack of emotional connection that might, in the long term, cause the relationship to be unsustainable.

FEARFUL-AVOIDANT & FEARFUL-AVOIDANT ATTACHMENT STYLE

Two Fearful-Avoidants in a relationship can create both immense passion and immense chaos. They both have strong emotional energy and a lot of fire. These two often bond deeply and intimately in the early stages of their relationship, creating an intoxicating high. Yet they often carry a lot of emotional baggage into relationships and are triggered easily.

The high of this sort of relationship is that there is strong, intense connection between the two when they feel they can be vulnerable. They share deeply, connect intensely, and are often extremely infatuated with one another.

On the flip side, there can be despair when one pulls away from the other. This relationship is highly volatile and, without the proper coping mechanisms, can be very difficult. In the following chapters there will be a breakdown on how the Fearful-Avoidant can heal their core wounds and become a wonderful, loving partner.

FEARFUL-AVOIDANT & SECURE ATTACHMENT STYLE

This dynamic is often very empowering for the Fearful-Avoidant if they allow themselves to be open to trusting their partner. It will begin with both parties deeply connecting, and the Fearful-Avoidant partner experiencing strong infatuation.

Over time, the Fearful-Avoidant might begin to withdraw when they feel too vulnerable. The Fearful-Avoidant also tends to sacrifice their needs in order to become worthy of love. This may create resentment over time, which can cause them to lash out at their Secure partner later on.

The Secure partner often doesn't give in to these protest behaviors. At best, the Fearful-Avoidant will learn to express their feelings and needs by modeling after their partner. They will learn to trust and still maintain deep connection.

At worst, the Fearful-Avoidant will rock the boat too much for their Secure Attachment partner. This can lead to the two splitting up, as the Secure is often excellent at sticking to their boundaries.

FEARFUL-AVOIDANT &
ANXIOUS ATTACHMENT STYLE

As mentioned previously, when they are willing to be vulnerable the Fearful-Avoidant can be an ideal partner for the Anxious Attachment. Since the Fearful-Avoidant has a strong subconscious drive to connect, it might feel as though their needs are being met in an ideal way.

However, at times the Fearful-Avoidant may feel overwhelmed by their Anxious Attachment partner. Sometimes they will feel smothered or distrustful. This can lead the Fearful-Avoidant to lash out emotionally and trigger their Anxious Attachment partner's wounds.

The Fearful-Avoidant often feels tremendous guilt after lashing out and comes back to the Anxious partner with apologies and promises. This can create a roller coaster for both partners.

Generally, this pairing can even bring out the more avoidant side of the Fearful-Avoidant. Their emotional volatility might diminish, but their need to withdraw and take time to themselves might increase.

The highs of this relationship can be intense connection and intoxicating closeness. However, the lows can include unpredictability for both parties. Argumentative behavior and difficulty communicating are not uncommon.

Ultimately, one or both parties will need to address their core wounds to have a healthier, happier relationship. Once this is done—as with all attachment style relationships—a wonderful bond can be created.

MY NOTES

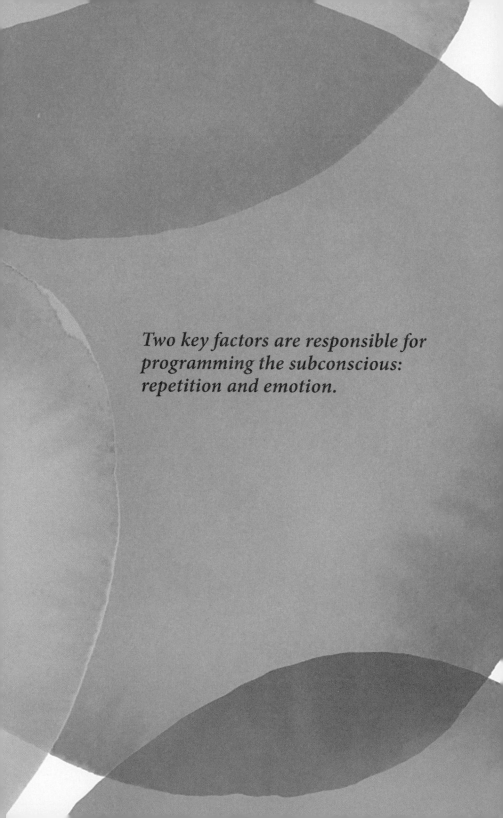

Two key factors are responsible for programming the subconscious: repetition and emotion.

Part 3

STRATEGIES FOR STRENGTHENING YOUR RELATIONSHIPS

Throughout this section of the book we will go through strategies and tools that will provide you with the ability to work through triggers and conflict within your relationships. We will be using a variety of different modalities and cognitive principles to deal with the common challenges that individuals face through their different attachment styles.

You will discover different views of conflict, gain new insights into why conflict might take place, and learn the steps to resolve it. These steps will be strategies you can use to find emotional relief independently or interdependently as you take new approaches to resolving the problems you face with others. It is recommended that you take the time to really soak in these tools, as they have the power to transform negative cycles and patterns in relationships if applied correctly.

It is advised that you use a pen and paper to note the obstacles that resonate with you in the examples we will be using. This is a great opportunity for furthering your self-awareness. You can follow this up by writing out the steps from the tools you will learn and applying them to the specific conflicts or challenges you find yourself facing within any relationship in your life. This can act as a guide to help you break through old patterns and feel more content and fulfilled with your loved ones.

Chapter 3

OVERCOMING NEGATIVE INTERACTIONS

In this chapter we will explore the benefits of overcoming negative interactions in the form of arguments, misunderstandings, and harbored resentment. Acceptance and Commitment Therapy is one way to cope with arguments with romantic partners, friends, or family members. It focuses on mindfulness strategies that help us move from a reactionary perspective into a reflective mind-set. By doing this, we are able to better identify how we feel and expend our own energy on positive solutions.

Throughout this chapter, we will focus on how two people in a romantic relationship overcome an argument. Imagine there is a Fearful-Avoidant named Aliyah and an Anxious Attachment named Lincoln. They continuously argue over Aliyah spending too much time away from home—at work, with friends, and so on. Recently, she was even late for their anniversary dinner. *So, what can Aliyah and Lincoln do to overcome their negative interactions?*

To begin to answer this question, the underlying associations that each partner has in the situation must be unpacked. From there, their needs can be examined and effective strategies can be created to meet those needs. Without understanding the fundamental forces at play for each individual, an effective and long-lasting solution cannot be found.

Step One: Observe Yourself

As described by the Association for Contextual Behavioral Science, *Acceptance and Commitment Therapy* (ACT) is a form of empirically based psychological intervention that focuses on mindfulness. *Mindfulness* is the state of focusing on the present to remove oneself from feeling consumed by the emotion experienced in the moment. To properly observe yourself, begin by noticing where in your body you experience emotion. For example, think about a time when you felt really sad. You may have felt despair in your chest, or a sense of hollowness in your stomach. If you were angry, you may have felt a burning sensation in your arms.

This occurs within everyone, in different variations. A study conducted by Carnegie Mellon University traced emotional responses in the brain to different activity signatures in the body through a functional magnetic resonance imaging (fMRI) scanner. If someone recalled a painful or traumatic memory, the prefrontal cortex and neocortex became less active, and their "reptilian brain" was activated. The former areas of the brain are responsible for conscious thought, spatial reasoning, and higher functions such as sensory perception. The latter is responsible for fight-or-flight responses. This means that the bodily responses caused by your emotions provide an opportunity for you to be mindful of them. Your emotions create sensations in your body that reflect your mind.

Dr. Bruce Lipton, a developmental biologist who studies gene expression in relation to environmental factors, released a study on epigenetics that sheds light on this matter. It revealed that an individual's body cannot heal when it is in its sympathetic state. The sympathetic nervous system, informally known as the fight-or-flight state, is triggered by certain emotional responses. This means that when we are *consumed* by emotion, an effective solution cannot be found until we shift our mind into *reflecting* on our emotions.

Let's take a moment and test this theory together. Try to focus on what you're feeling and where, and this will ground you in the present moment. By focusing on how you are responding, you essentially remove yourself from being consumed by your emotions in that moment. This brings you back into your sensory perception and moves the response in your brain back into the cortex and neocortex. This transition helps bring you back into a more logical state where emotions are not controlling your reactions.

Recall Aliyah and Lincoln's argument over her presence in the relationship. Imagine she is late to her anniversary dinner with Lincoln because she had a very important work deadline that she had to meet that evening. For Lincoln, the Anxious Attachment, Aliyah's tardiness triggers his core fear of abandonment. He feels incredibly anxious, and adrenaline radiates throughout his body as he wonders if Aliyah's distance is a result of a shift in her feelings. However, Aliyah feels overwhelmed by Lincoln's clinginess and recoils. For the Fearful-Avoidant, an abundance of emotional connection feels unsafe. In the moment, both forget that their response is a result of the core wounds that their attachment style perpetuates.

However, despite the strong response in his reptilian brain, Lincoln remembers that he is supposed to witness and label his emotions. He asks himself: *Where am I feeling my emotional response in my body?* He identifies that he is feeling anger and fear in his arms and legs. By witnessing and labeling these emotions, he brings his brain back into a state of higher functioning, and his neocortex and cortex begin to reactivate. The simple act of witnessing and labelling his emotions allows him to stop being *reactive* and brings him into a state of *reflection*. This is the first step to practice while shifting into an ACT approach.

Although it may seem straightforward to witness your emotions, some find it difficult at first because they have been living their whole lives viewing their emotions as an automatic, uncontrollable response rather than as information. The act of witnessing your emotions is important in all aspects and areas of your life, not just in arguments with friends or significant others. Without witnessing emotions, you are at their mercy—rather than taking the chance to *learn* from them and inquire about what they're trying to tell you.

Emotions can even have a widespread physiological impact. In his book *In the Realm of Hungry Ghosts*, Dr. Gabor Maté, a physician who specializes in childhood development and trauma, researched the ways in which guilt affects physiology. He claimed that guilt is a persistent emotion that creates a subconscious "nest" that the mind retreats to when an individual has done something wrong. Rather than guilt being a direct response to something, it is a continuous belief that runs in the background and elicits a physiological response. This then reinforces negative subconscious beliefs and perpetuates an unhealthy cycle of thinking. Physiologically, it is an emotion that releases hormones that weaken the immune system, contribute to depression, put stress on cardiac muscles, and ultimately shorten your lifespan. The fact that just one emotion has been scientifically proven to so deeply impact an individual's physiology speaks to the importance of recognizing and labeling emotions. Think of the implications of all the emotions we have daily—especially when the average person has between 60,000 and 70,000 thoughts per day! Not only is witnessing your emotions a tool that effectively places you in a reflective mind-set, but it is a tool that can drastically improve the quality of your life.

Step Two: Identify Unmet Needs

Conflict is largely the result of unmet needs that we aren't consciously aware of.

Once you have witnessed your emotions, you need to ask yourself why they are there. *What unmet need are they expressing to you?* Aliyah and Lincoln both have unmet needs that they are struggling to express to themselves *and* to one another.

How do we identify our unmet needs? Begin by considering your primary attachment style. Since each attachment style has underlying conflicts and subconscious beliefs that they are perpetuating, consider what voids have existed in your life. This can be done with each attachment style and can reveal what underlying triggers are contributing to the conflict at hand. Only once our unmet needs are identified can we begin to create strategies to meet them.

Fearful-Avoidant Needs

Aliyah, a Fearful-Avoidant, can be examined first. Recall that Fearful-Avoidants had incongruency in their childhood, which was often paired with some form of abuse—whether it be physical, emotional, or sexual. Typically, they had some sort of emotional connection with one or both caregivers, who were also a victim to, or the perpetrator of, pain. They began to associate emotional connection with a lack of safety, and thus developed a strong aversion to vulnerability. However, humans are biologically hardwired to seek connection. For the Fearful-Avoidant, this creates a strong need for emotional connection in conjunction with a sense of safety.

In all relationships, the Fearful-Avoidant will have core wounds that surround a feeling of impending betrayal and a strong sense of fear. They subconsciously believe that they will be taken advantage of and that they're unworthy of those around them. Therefore, they need a partner who is predictable and will provide a safe connection while respecting their boundaries. Their partner must also be very forthcoming in order to show the Fearful-Avoidant that vulnerability can be safe.

Aliyah, in this instance, would need Lincoln to respect her boundaries while reassuring her that it is okay to pursue her career. This would open up a line of communication between the two as Aliyah would feel supported, and she would likely be more mindful of Lincoln's feelings in the future rather than recoiling.

Anxious Attachment Needs

The Anxious Attachment has altogether different needs than the Fearful-Avoidant. The Anxious Attachment, who constantly fears abandonment, needs constant reassurance. They feel a sense of emotional hunger due to their inability to self-soothe as a child. When they feel an emotional connection, they will overcompensate to maintain it. Their core wounds revolve around the idea that they will be rejected, unloved, and excluded. They need a partner who is affectionate, reassuring, and predictable.

Unfortunately, the behavior often exhibited by an Anxious Attachment who is unaware of their needs frequently exacerbates issues in the relationship. For Lincoln, his frustration with Aliyah's unpredictable presence only pushes her away. Without identifying that he needs a partner who is reliable because of his subconscious fear of abandonment, he cannot properly express this to her and will alternately be resentful and argumentative. To properly communicate with Aliyah, he must help her to understand that what he needs is different than what she needs. He needs to know that she will always be there for him—regardless of what her work or friendships demand.

Ultimately, the argument is not actually about Aliyah being late to dinner. The argument is instead about Aliyah feeling as though she cannot handle the pressure to be vulnerable in the relationship and Lincoln feeling as though he will be abandoned. In this scenario, they both have unmet needs that result from their attachment styles' core wounds. Without identifying these needs, they cannot effectively communicate with each other and will face difficulty overcoming their relationship challenges.

Dismissive-Avoidant Needs

Although this style is outside the scope of the Aliyah-Lincoln anecdote, the Dismissive-Avoidant has their own needs. The Dismissive-Avoidant suffered from moderate to severe emotional neglect as a child, and therefore their subconscious was taught to be autonomous and self-sufficient. Their core wounds revolve around vulnerability feeling painful and feeling a sense of defectiveness. Therefore, their needs in relationships include direct communication and unwavering support.

Key Points to Remember

Needs do not only stem from your attachment style. *Personality needs* are the subconscious strategies you've programmed with the most positive—over negative—associations to getting your six basic human needs met.

According to the Habits of Well-Being, from the work of Tony Robbins, the six basic human needs are:

1. Love and connection
2. Significance
3. Certainty
4. Uncertainty
5. Growth
6. Contribution

They are the basis of the choices we make and are fundamental to success and happiness.

The first four of the six needs are what are called *Needs of the Personality*. They help define the human sense of achievement:

1. Love and connection is the need for attachment
2. Significance is the need to have meaning
3. Certainty is the need for safety or control
4. Uncertainty is the need for challenges or excitement

The remaining two needs are what are known as *Needs of the Spirit*.

1. Growth is the need for intellectual or spiritual development
2. Contribution is the need to give beyond ourselves

Needs are also paradoxical. With more challenges come less certainty, and more value placed on a search for deeper meaning often comes at the cost of less intimate connection with others. Within the spiritual needs, more growth comes with less contribution. By considering these needs in conjunction with the voids created by your attachment style, you can therefore *begin to understand your most important needs and your unmet needs*. For example, as an Anxious Attachment, you may value the basic human need of love and connection more so than significance. By overlaying the Robbins theory with attachment theory, one can begin to identify their subconscious needs and which ones are unmet.

The combination of Tony Robbins's teachings and attachment theory can be taken one step further—to illustrate that the void in your attachment style that creates resonance with certain basic human needs then goes on to form your identity. For example, Aliyah is a Fearful-Avoidant who resonates strongly with the need for growth because through career growth she attains a sense of worthiness (recall that unworthiness is a core wound of the Fearful-Avoidant). She then begins to identify as an achiever. Essentially, she has the unmet need of career achievement because the abuse she endured as a child has caused her subconscious to believe that it is unworthy. As an adult, Aliyah *needs* to excel in her career because success fills the void created by her parents, which caused her to feel she was unworthy. Then, to meet this self-identification, tertiary needs become involved.

Tertiary needs are the day-to-day actions that help fill the void, or core wounds, created by parenting during childhood. For Aliyah, this means she needs support for her career and validation from her partner. These are the actions she requires from her partner to feel as though the relationship is healthy.

In summary, we come to see that every action is a subconscious strategy to get our needs met, yet we can only meet these needs once we trace them back to their origins and identify them.

To identify them, begin by looking at what your attachment style is.

- Ask yourself: *What are your core wounds?* They will be along the lines of "I am unworthy," "I am unlovable," "vulnerability is unsafe," and so on.

- Next, look at which of the six basic human needs these core wounds drive you toward. If you feel unlovable, you may place a high value on love and connection. If you're like Aliyah and feel unworthy, you may place a high value on significance.

- Then, ask yourself: *What does this make me identify as?* If you subconsciously believe you are unlovable and have found you've attained love from relationships, you may come to know yourself as a "relationship person." This is because, through relationships, you are attempting to heal the core wound of feeling unlovable.

Ultimately, this is what makes up your identity, and your day-to-day, or tertiary, needs from a partner will be what speaks to your identity and, ultimately, your core subconscious wounds.

Step Three: Create Strategies to Get These Needs Met

Now that you are aware of how to observe your emotions and then identify your needs, the key question comes up: *How do I get these needs met?*

Clear Communication

The first way to do this properly and intuitively is to find out what your needs truly are and then communicate them. Although this seems straightforward, this may mean different things to different attachment styles. The Dismissive-Avoidant, for example, needs clear communication. They get frustrated and withdraw when they are expected to read between the lines. To communicate clearly in a relationship, regardless of whether it is a friendship or a romantic relationship, begin by asking your partner what communication means to them. Also ask yourself what communication means to you.

For Aliyah, communication is likely a combination of discussion and having her boundaries honored during the discussion. Since she is fearful of vulnerability, it is essential that Lincoln holds space for the discussion and respects if she wants to take a break from talking before resuming later.

From start to finish, here is how the disagreement may progress to the point of getting her needs met:

1. When Aliyah starts yelling at Lincoln about him not understanding that she *had* to be late to meet her work deadline, she should first ask herself where she is feeling her anger in her body.
   - This shifts her outside of her reptilian brain and into her cortex where she can begin to experience higher-level thinking.
   - This is the first ACT mindfulness technique.

2. Once she is in a state of reflection rather than reactivity, she can witness her emotions.
   - She can then ask herself: *Why am I feeling this way? What are my emotions trying to tell me?*
   - Her anger, for example, is telling her that in this situation she has a need that is unmet by

Lincoln, and this need is originating from a core wound.

- Generally, the stronger we feel about a situation that is relatively small, such as being late for dinner, the more negatively stored associations we have subconsciously.

3. Then, she can identify what that unmet need is.
   - From a tertiary and personality-needs level, it is feeling as though she is unsupported in her journey to achievement.
   - However, this is not the core wound—it is only the needs that are not being met.
   - She can then ask herself: *Why am I so strongly triggered about being unsupported? What does that mean about me?*
   - She can then identify that it means that she feels unworthy, and that her achievement is what is being used to define her identity.

4. The core wound for Aliyah, which is feeling unworthy, is what was brought about by the way she was treated as a child. This treatment is what created her Fearful-Avoidant attachment style.

Working through this process and answering these questions is what allows an individual to realize what their needs are and to better communicate them to their partners, friends, or family. Aliyah would then be able to tell Lincoln that she feels that he is not supporting her, which is especially painful because she has always felt unworthy. To meet her needs, she can clearly communicate to him that she needs him to support her in this journey and to understand that her ambition is not her abandoning him—it is her trying to fill the void of her core wound.

To clearly communicate needs, you must first understand them. Then, ensure you know *how* to express your needs for your partner to understand them. From there, you can have an open dialogue and work toward meeting each other's needs in a more enlightened way.

However, communication is not the only piece required to get needs met. Energy must be invested in working toward a positive solution instead of fighting against the problem. Interestingly enough, fighting against existing problems not only prevents us from getting our needs met, but also perpetuates suffering.

Firstly, the past is fundamentally static. Once it has occurred, arguing does nothing but prevent people from investing their energy into finding a collective solution that gets their needs met. The moment that Aliyah was late for dinner, nothing could be done to change it. Arguing about it prevented both individuals from getting their needs met—they were giving their energy to nothing. Why do people do this? It occurs because they were trying to get their needs met without knowing it. For example, Aliyah's core wound of being unworthy and unsafe is triggered—by arguing, she is subconsciously attempting to regain a sense of control. Yet she can do this in a more productive manner by communicating to Lincoln *why* she was late, what needs she was trying to meet, and how he in turn he can meet those needs. Ultimately, the subconscious makes decisions before the conscious mind, and it does so when it perceives more benefits than drawbacks. Open dialogue will manage expectations in the relationship and help surface the underlying causes of the choices that contributed to this situation. Moreover, their energy will be invested in a positive way, rather than it being used to fight against the past. Once needs are identified, they can be met by focusing on the solution rather than the problem.

Last, in order to get their needs met, both partners need to know the difference between being mindful versus sacrificing. They need to ask themselves whether certain aspects of the relationship can realistically be changed and at what cost. Without recognizing his needs, Lincoln, for example, would likely self-sacrifice to keep Aliyah happy in an attempt to soothe his core fear of abandonment. This would include accepting her continued absence and internalizing the resentment that he feels as a result. This would damage the relationship and must be avoided. However, if Lincoln were to go through the same process as Aliyah did—beginning with witnessing her bodily response to her emotions—he, too, could identify his needs and find compromise *rather than sacrifice*. For Lincoln, an Anxious Attachment, it would include him asking that she take the occasional night off, while respecting that she may need to work late some nights.

The difference between sacrifice and compromise is important, especially if you are still learning what your core wounds are. Without proper identification, trade-offs that are motivated by your subconscious could end up creating turmoil in your relationships. In conclusion, by first witnessing, then inquiring, and then communicating, negative interactions can be sublimated and needs met effectively.

WRAP-UP

By distilling ACT techniques, incorporating some aspects of Tony Robbins's theories, and mixing in my own experience with thousands of individuals, I created a unique approach to need-meeting. Now that you have the information about the processes required to get your needs met in a relationship, how do you think Lincoln determines what his needs are? How does he get them met by Aliyah?

For some help figuring out how Lincoln would do so, answer these questions:

- If you were Lincoln, where would you feel the anger in your body?

- What are these emotions trying to tell him?

- What are these emotions telling him about his unmet needs as an Anxious Attachment? For example, it may be that he is unlovable.

- How does this reflect what he needs from a personality and tertiary-needs perspective? It may be along the lines of needing support because he is a "relationship man."

- How can he get these needs met by Aliyah, and how will he communicate this?

By examining Lincoln and Aliyah in this framework, we can see that eventually they will come to a deeper and longer-lasting solution. They will open a more encapsulating dialogue and remove some of the challenges from the relationship.

But how does this framework apply to you? Consider a recent argument with a friend, partner, or family member.

- *What does that negative interaction tell you about yourself?*

- *What steps would you take to understand your needs in this situation and get them met?*

Write down the process for yourself.

Keep in mind this chapter is about managing negative interactions. To understand how to actually *heal* the core wounds that are creating those interactions, check out the next chapter!

ACT Techniques to Help

There are techniques that can help you implement ACT into your daily life in small but meaningful ways. See the options below to find out how.

- **Start Your Morning Right.** Your brain is the most susceptible to suggestion when you first wake up and right before you go to bed. Beginning your morning by witnessing how you feel and why you feel that way can therefore help set the tone for the rest of the day. For example, if you feel like you woke up on the wrong side of the bed, your subconscious actually becomes hyper-sensitive to negative events throughout the day as a means of protecting yourself. Consider why you feel this way, and by being mindful of your feelings you can effectively shape your perceptions for the rest of the day.

- **Focus on the Little Things.** This can range from monitoring your body language to noticing how your shoes feel on your feet. Small observations that ground you in the present help shift your brain in the ways discussed in this chapter. By being mindful of such things, you better prepare yourself to inquire about what you need today.

- **Ask Yourself What You Need Today.** This is perhaps the most important tip for your day. By taking a moment to identify what needs you have and *why*, you set yourself up to get them met. The next step is to properly communicate your needs and to hold space for others trying to do the same.

By implementing these small tips and tricks, the extent to which you see a positive change may surprise you. Considering the magnitude of thoughts we have daily, even making small changes like the ones mentioned above can have a cascading effect on your well-being. Remember, the goal is ultimately to shift your attachment style to a more Secure place in your relationships, and to do so, you must first be mindful of how you feel and what your needs are.

Chapter 4

CHANGING YOUR OUTLOOK

This chapter will explore the ways in which Cognitive Behavioral Therapy (CBT) techniques can be applied to difficult situations to relieve emotional suffering. Moreover, by taking a more intensive approach than that tradition-ally outlined in CBT, you can look at the core subconscious beliefs that you are projecting onto a situation and which may be causing undue pain. This approach allows you to truly create long-lasting change in all areas of your life and helps you to truly address the underlying wounds that your attachment style may exhibit.

The approach that I have created follows a series of steps that draw on fundamental aspects of CBT, as well as the trends I have seen in thousands of clients. It is as follows:

- Begin by reflecting on the situation and identifying emotional patterns.

- Ask yourself what meaning is being assigned to the situation and what core wound it activates.

- Look for proof of the opposite and reflect.

To better illustrate this approach, two co-workers will serve as a demonstration in this chapter: Suneel, a Fearful-Avoidant, and Connor, a Dismissive-Avoidant. They are unable to work effectively together because they are giving meaning to an argument that is being projected from their subconsciouses. Without realizing this and healing their core wounds, their work relationship and output will deteriorate rapidly.

Reflect on the Situation

Cognitive Behavioral Therapy (CBT) is a form of therapy that focuses on changing unfavorable thought patterns. By taking a deeper approach to traditional CBT, I have created an outline for you to follow based on your core subconscious beliefs.

Begin by reflecting on the situation: Use the same mindfulness techniques mentioned in the previous chapter, such as witnessing your emotions or meditating. By being mindful, you give your brain the opportunity to switch into a state that allows it to better process its emotions. From here, subconscious triggers can clearly be identified. Under traditional CBT, being mindful helps identify what are known as *automatic thoughts.* These are the ideas that flow into the brain seemingly on autopilot: The conscious mind does not give much thought to them, and they are the "fillers" of your day-to-day thoughts. We are going to look at the subconscious programs that actually create those thoughts. The subconscious is responsible for about 90 percent of the brain's functionality, and the stored associations and beliefs that exist within the subconscious are what perpetuate conscious thoughts. This is an especially important notion when considering triggers.

But, what do we mean when we label something as a trigger? When we discuss triggers within this text, we are referring to a topic or event that provokes or recalls negative emotion. Since the subconscious mind is programmed through repetition and emotion at a conscious *and* subconscious level, anything experienced alongside a strong combination of the two will affect the way that reality is perceived. For example, consider the work relationship between Suneel and Connor. Suneel is a Fearful-Avoidant and Connor is a Dismissive-Avoidant. They are working together on a project that has a looming deadline, yet they continually disagree with each other's approaches to the work. *How do their triggers make this situation exceedingly difficult, and what do their attachment styles have to do with it?*

As a child, Suneel experienced emotional abuse from parents who were manipulative. Connor was neglected most of his childhood since his parents were preoccupied with work. Connor eventually began to believe, subconsciously, that he was defective in some way—parental absence made him feel unworthy and alone. As an adult, he can be characterized as a Dismissive-Avoidant. Repeatedly feeling alone as a child is what programmed his subconscious to believe that he is unworthy. Scenarios that relate to that emotion are therefore a deep core wound for Connor, and he will become triggered. As an adult, when Suneel criticizes Connor's approach, Connor subconsciously relives the experience of feeling emotionally neglected and unworthy of his parents' love. In this moment, his subconscious feels unworthy of his job because his work is seemingly not good enough. It becomes an experience that is disproportionally painful to the actual situation at hand.

> *An important aspect to note about triggers is that although the triggered feelings are real, the thoughts, beliefs, and assumptions surrounding the triggers may not be an accurate representation of what is actually happening.*

On the other hand, Suneel feels uncomfortable with vulnerability because as a child he learned to associate it with pain. When he shares his opinion with Connor and is met with disdain and anger, he therefore withdraws and feels incredibly frustrated. He has automatic thoughts such as: "Connor is a terrible person to work with," and "Why is that guy such a mean person?" Connor has automatic thoughts such as: "Suneel is not good at his job. His opinion is wrong, and we'll never get this project done." As you can see, attachment styles have key subconscious triggers that occur because of the repetition of a specific emotion at a young age. These core wounds are then what produce automatic thoughts that must be witnessed to avoid perpetuating outdated beliefs. In reality, Suneel has a different opinion that can help advance the project, and Connor's work built a great foundation to begin with, yet the core wounds that underlie both individuals create unnecessary and painful conflicts.

Often, our emotions lead us to believe that the problem at hand is unsolvable when in reality the true problem is not properly identified. Begin by isolating and identifying the actual emotional challenge. *What needs are unmet in this situation?* For Connor, from a tertiary perspective, it is support and validation. For Suneel, it would be respect and the safety to express his opinions. *What meaning is being given to the situation?* Again, for Connor it would be that he is unworthy. For Suneel, it would be that vulnerability is unsafe. By taking a moment to witness the strong emotions, we can identify the core wound that causes the response. It is essential to remember that our emotions are here to serve us—they are like alarm bells that are telling us a core wound is being triggered and our needs are unmet. To better illustrate this concept, consider how you feel when you are hungry. Hunger is a feeling that exists to elicit a response out of us. It is telling us that we need to be fed. Other emotions act in the same manner—they exist to elicit a change that will help us.

Once an emotional trigger is identified, certain trigger patterns in your life will begin to emerge. The same feeling of unworthiness for Connor occurs in his romantic relationships when his partner gets angry at him, and with his parents when they are too busy to see him. This elicits an angry response that he sees across his daily life. The same patterns also emerge for Suneel. It is essential to begin identifying emotional trigger patterns because once we familiarize ourselves with them, we can begin to remove their emotional charge. Think about it like this: *If someone were to ask you to walk through a house that you've never been through before, with the lights off, and not to bump into anything, could you do it?* Of course not. This is because it is unfamiliar, and we do not know what exists in the house. However, if you were to go through the house with the lights on first before walking through the dark, it would be an immense help for navigation. Subconscious triggers work in the same way—although they are a challenge, once we recognize and decode them, we can handle them better in everyday life.

Ultimately, it is important to delve deeper into our triggered automatic thoughts, as they elicit an emotional response that is here to tell us something. It is telling us that there is a subconscious core wound that needs to be recognized so that it does not come out unfavorably in everyday life.

Ask yourself:

- *What meaning are you giving to the situation?*

- *Can you know it is completely true?* For example: Can Connor really know that Suneel is a fundamentally mean, terrible coworker?

- Or is his subconscious assigning this meaning to the situation automatically because he is triggered emotionally?

Taking a moment to be mindful of the emotions that arise during a situation is the first step to uncovering the deeper meaning that lies in certain circumstances.

Automatic Thoughts and Finding Evidence

Automatic thoughts occur because the subconscious mind stores information that is meant to protect you. However, it also stores negative associations better than positive ones because it acts as a safety mechanism. Although this is effective from an evolutionary standpoint, it unfortunately perpetuates a lot of anxious and hopeless thoughts. Also keep in mind that since the subconscious mind is pro-grammed through repetition and emotion, the more we perpetuate beliefs, the more deeply ingrained they become over time.

So, how do we identify automatic thoughts and the core triggers that created them? Well, the brain is always looking for information to support what it believes. This is called *supportive evidence*. Supportive evidence is the information that the brain picks out of its environment to reinforce its existing thoughts. In the context of reprogramming your subconscious, this is a negative practice. An example of this may occur if Connor were to go to a work party—remember that he believes that he is fundamentally unworthy of emo-tional connection. When he walks in, his automatic thoughts include "No one likes me, and no one wants me here." The brain then begins to look for supportive evidence: Someone frowning in conversation while looking in his direction, to Connor, means that they hate him and want him to leave. With Suneel, supportive evidence may occur when Suneel makes grammatical corrections in the project they're working on together. To Connor, this may again reinforce that Suneel is trying to undermine him.

A powerful aspect of supportive evidence to consider is that it occurs every day and everywhere in our lives. Our mind is constantly looking for supportive evidence of what our subconscious believes. When the subconscious stores fundamentally painful beliefs, they become projected onto our reality everywhere we look. Therefore, it is essential to begin looking for *contradictory evidence* for our core wounds to reprogram our subconscious and heal our everyday perspectives.

Contradictory evidence is information that disproves existing beliefs. Since memory is colored by emotion, finding contradictory evidence in our past and present and pairing it with the emotions associated with that experience allows us to begin reprogramming our subconscious. Essentially, finding *proof of the opposite* helps to equilibrate our subconscious, and from there, it can be taught new and updated beliefs. To better understand what this means, consider the circumstances that Suneel and Connor are experiencing. Connor, who believes he is unworthy, should begin by considering where in the *seven primary areas of life* this belief has been proven otherwise.

The seven primary areas of life are:

1. Family

2. Spiritual

3. Financial

4. Mental/Emotional

5. Career

6. Physical

7. Social

Connor may begin by recalling when he placed in the top ten of a marathon in the previous year and was worthy of that physical achievement. He should also remember when he connected with his best friend last month over a difficult experience and felt worthy of his friend's attention and time. By finding contradictory evidence of his subconscious mind's core beliefs, he can begin to emotionally equilibrate. This then reduces the amount that his subconscious mind produces automatic thoughts surrounding a sense of unworthiness. His everyday interactions become healthier, and his perspectives will shift into a better space.

For Suneel, vulnerability feels threatening. It makes him, at his core, feel unsafe. Therefore, Suneel must look for times in all areas of his life where this is contradictory. For example, it could be the time last week where he discussed a raise with his boss and was promised a new contract. When Suneel began to commit himself more deeply to his religion by getting more involved with his church, he once again proved that being vulnerable with others can be safe. Like Connor, Suneel must find similar contradictory evidence in all areas of his life to begin neutralizing his emotional reactions. At this point, both individuals better understand what their core wounds are, what emotional patterns they elicit, and how to begin equilibrating them. This puts them in a significantly better—and less reactive—position to complete their project prior to their deadline and improve their overall emotional well-being.

A helpful question to ask yourself when considering your automatic thoughts is: *What meaning am I giving to this situation, and can I absolutely know this is true?* Most of the time, negative thoughts and triggers are rooted in outdated beliefs that were created in childhood. By beginning to uproot these beliefs and heal our perceptions, we can begin to move toward a more Secure Attachment in all our relationships.

Identify Fair and Balanced Thoughts

As you begin the journey into your thoughts, you'll likely notice that there are patterns into which your mind likes to distort your thinking. In CBT, there are common types of cognitive distortions, or patterns, into which your thinking can skew your perception of reality.

While reading the following paragraphs, take the time to notice which cognitive distortions in your patterns of thinking you experience the most. Following the suggestions in the follow-up solutions, strategize thought upgrades that would work best for you in returning your thinking to a fair and balanced perspective.

The idea here is to be able to release one-sided distortions in your thinking and replace them with practical, reasonable thoughts that empower you to focus on the solution instead of constantly exacerbating the problem or challenge you face.

All-or-Nothing Thinking

This type of cognitive distortion occurs when we view the world in black and white or in extremes. As this type of distortion shows up in our thoughts, it can also show up in our behaviors.

Let's imagine there is a woman named Stacy who is dating a man named Jack. One evening, after two years of dating, Jack says he will call Stacy but forgets to do so. Stacy calls Jack the next day and says, "You forgot to call me and now I can never trust you again to do what you promise."

This would be an example of all-or-nothing thinking. Stacy believes that because Jack made a mistake once, he will always make this mistake and cannot be trusted in a relationship. Not only do Stacy's thoughts hurt her, but they have the potential to hurt Jack as well.

A good solution here would be for Stacy to communicate her concerns, without thinking in black and white. She might say to Jack, "I am hurt that you forgot to call and I am concerned about your ability to follow through on your commitments. It is important to me that you treat our commitments with more care."

Stacy might remind herself that, while Jack made a mistake, mistakes are bound to happen at times in a relationship. Jack's mistake in one area doesn't necessarily translate to him being untrustworthy in all areas of the relationship. What matters most is that Stacy communicates her concerns and gives Jack an opportunity to apologize and make a change. This would be an example of returning to a fair and balanced perspective. Should this situation consistently repeat itself, this would be a different story.

Catastrophizing

Catastrophizing is a cognitive distortion that leads to diving down the rabbit hole of fear. It is when the mind constantly ruminates over the absolute worst-case scenarios in life.

Let's imagine Mateo and Jacob have been dating for six months. One weekend, Mateo and Jacob are supposed to go away together and Mateo cancels at the last minute. Jacob starts panicking. He begins to think thoughts like, "Mateo doesn't want to be with me. He is only with me out of pity. He is about to leave the relationship and I'll never find anyone again. I always knew I would be alone forever."

These are very painful thoughts. Jacob plays an entire movie in his mind, imagining himself in scenes where he is much older and lonely, without anyone to speak to. As our minds have a challenging time telling the difference between what is real and what is imagined, Jacob feels emotionally drained by his thinking. He also produces enormous amounts of cortisol when his physiological responses respond to these thoughts.

Catastrophizing can create an enormous amount of anxiety and can deeply impact our relationships. How do you think Jacob treats Mateo when he speaks to him next? Jacob is much less likely to be himself and will probably be triggered into expressing the unhealthy side of his attachment style.

An important solution for this is for Jacob to practice questioning his thoughts. He can ask himself, "Do I truly know this is a fact? Is it possible that Mateo might have canceled for another reason?" Jacob can also ask for clarification from Mateo after he has questioned the original story that he has told himself.

By questioning the story, Jacob can return to a fair and balanced perspective. He can recognize that it is impossible to know for certain what his future will be, or why Mateo canceled. This can lead him to the much healthier behavior of seeking clarification in order to release some of the self-created stress instigated by his thought patterns.

Labeling

In CBT, labeling is the act of judging a mistake or behavior as a character trait. Labeling often produces self-defeating internal dialogue.

Let's use the example of Andrew, who makes a mistake while turning in a report at work. When Andrew realizes he did this, he exclaims to himself, "I am such an idiot! Only losers do things like this. What a loser everyone will think I am."

Andrew judges a mistake as an intrinsic character flaw. This is a huge cognitive distortion. It is also self-diminishing and can lower self-esteem. The way you speak to yourself in your mind plays an important role in the way you feel about yourself.

Andrew's thoughts and perceptions literally create emotional and neurochemical responses. When he falls into the trap of labeling himself, he will feel more inadequate and incapable than the mistake already made him feel.

An important solution here is to practice separating behaviors from character traits. This empowers you to shift your negative patterns of self-criticism as well as correct the behavior once you notice it. You can go so far as trying to understand the root cause of the behavior and trying to create strategies to prevent it from occurring again.

For example, if Andrew wasn't so busy beating himself up in his thinking, he would be more likely to recognize that he made a mistake because he was rushing. He would then be empowered to create a new strategy to better manage his time and work toward solving problems at their root. Labeling not only hurt Andrew, but it prevented him from expanding his self-awareness in the situation, limiting his capacity to grow.

Overgeneralization

This is the propensity to make one experience constitute *all* experiences. It is easy to do this when feeling discouraged or frustrated but is a very painful cognitive distortion that prevents one from effectively growing and moving through challenges.

Let's look at Pari's example to illustrate this. Pari wants to settle down and get married and has just returned from a first date. She met someone named Sam who was late to the date and didn't express much interest in her. Pari gets home and calls her friend to discuss the details of the date. She says to her friend, "The date didn't go well.

Sam wasn't very interested, and I just know now that nobody will be interested in me. I'm so disappointed and I hate dating. All dates are so uncomfortable."

Pari assumes that because one date didn't go well, all dates will not go well. She uses one experience to make a generalization about dating in general. She even goes as far as to say, "All dates are so uncomfortable." This prevents Pari from having a fair chance at finding someone, as she is going in with a self-defeating outlook and is likely to feel more insecure or uncomfortable on future dates.

An important strategy here is to actively practice separating one experience from *all* experiences. If you notice yourself using words like "always" or "never," this is a sign that you are overgeneralizing. This can be painful when we generalize traits about our partner or loved ones as well.

Some other important cognitive distortions include mind-reading, fortune-telling, and personalization. With mind-reading, you assume you know what others are thinking. Fortune-telling is the act of making assumptions about the future that produce negative emotion. Personalization is the act of assuming blame or fault for any situation that takes place. An example of this would be getting upset at yourself if your child gets hurt during recess at school.

Take some time to write down which cognitive distortions are most prominent for you. *Which ones cause you the most grief or unhealthy habits in your relationships?* Follow up by using the strategies described above to return to a fair and balanced perspective. You will know you have reached this place because you will feel as though your emotional charge around the situations has lessened and you are operating from a grounded, realistic frame of mind.

Monitor Your Present Mood

After reading the previous segments, it is important to reflect on how you feel. Think about automatic thoughts you may have had over this past week, and what core triggers may have caused them.

- *How did it feel when you believed thoughts like "I am unworthy" or "I am unlovable"?*

- *How did it feel when your brain identified supporting evidence?*

After completing the exercise of looking at the seven areas of your life, ask yourself: *How do I feel now?* By looking for proof of the opposite, you will eventually be able to neutralize the charge you have placed on a specific core belief. From there, you can begin to teach your subconscious a more updated perspective based on how your life is *today*. For example, if you are in a loving relationship today, it may have taught you that emotional vulnerability *is* safe and that you *are* lovable.

Given this information, the professional relationship between Suneel and Connor can be further examined—assuming they both followed the same steps of identifying, questioning, and neutralizing. Once they had neutralized their core wounds, they were both more open to criticism and different perspectives. This opened lines of communication between them and allowed their project to flow more efficiently. Additionally, this drastically improved the ways they felt in every other aspect of their life. It is important to remember that every day our subconscious is taking in new information. Thus, our attachment styles can still be molded in adulthood by significantly emotional events or one type of event that is less emotionally challenging but occurs consistently. Therefore, it is important to both constantly question our thoughts and to look for other old or new core wounds that may arise. We are in a constant state of evolution and improvement and must prepare our mind for just that.

Moreover, after neutralizing the subconscious charge on a core belief, it is important to reflect on your mood at that moment. By doing so, you are continuing to practice mindfulness while working toward more positive habits.

This deeper approach to CBT will give you the tools to navigate through difficult situations in everyday life, improve your outlook, and help negotiate triggering scenarios. CBT at a surface level has had an astounding impact on the lives of millions of people. It helps to connect the beliefs, thoughts, physical responses, and behavior of individuals. By examining it at a subconscious level, the root of the beliefs can be revealed and healed.

Keep in mind that this process will differ between each attachment style since each style inherently has different triggers. For example, the Anxious Attachment, who was not mentioned anecdotally in this section, often has triggers surrounding being rejected, abandoned, or not good enough. Therefore, in scenarios that resurface these beliefs, the Anxious Attachment will automatically look for proof that these beliefs will happen. They will interpret late work nights as an emotional shift in their partner and missed phone calls as proof of impending abandonment. Eventually, these beliefs can become all-consuming and can harm the relationship. Therefore, the Anxious Attachment needs to look for examples of when, for example, their partner worked late but came home with their favorite take-out food. It is essential to find multiple examples where they *were* secure in a relationship. From there, they will be in a space where they can monitor their present mood. This is an essential last step to CBT and will help the Anxious Attachment recognize emotional patterns in the future.

There are also certain techniques that can help you ground yourself and examine your emotional patterns in everyday life. Meditation is a good example, since it allows you to observe your thoughts from a neutral space. Begin practicing mediation either when you wake up or before bed for optimal results. Whether it is a walk in the evening that allows you to reflect on your day or an open-ended discussion with your partner, ensure that you are adequately reflecting on the journey you have taken to work through an emotional trigger. This will help you repeat this process in the future as needed and will make you better attuned to when you feel triggered and what your emotions are trying to tell you in all areas of life.

WRAP-UP

In conclusion, if Suneel and Connor reflect on the core wounds that are creating tension in their relationship, they will be able to work together more effectively and meet their work deadline. If they are unable to do so, they will perpetuate outdated beliefs that cause undue pain and inaccurately perceive every kind of relationship in their lives. It is imperative to dig deeper than is normal in traditional CBT in order to get down to the subconscious root of automatic thoughts. From there, they must be questioned and neutralized. This process is what prepares your mind for updated beliefs, and it must be continually reflected upon and monitored as you go through life.

Since individuals also often express different attachment styles in different relationships due to the experiences that are associated with each relationship, core wounds may differ in distinct areas of life. Therefore, it is beneficial to reflect upon your emotional patterns in each kind of relationship you have, whether they are romantic, platonic, or familial. Also, have a conversation with your partner or friend about the meaning *they're* giving to certain conflicts. It can be surprising what associations they have stored in their subconscious and the miscommunication that subsequently goes on in their arguments.

By taking the time to adequately question your beliefs and remove yourself from autopilot, immense change can be seen in your life.

Daily Ways to Implement CBT

There are multiple ways to implement CBT in your daily life outside of an in-depth subconscious reprogram. Recall that the purpose of CBT is to uproot beliefs that no longer serve you in a positive way. Therefore, to implement CBT daily, look for techniques that allow you to reflect on yourself and your experiences more objectively.

Here are some examples:

- **Journaling.** Writing things down not only ensures that memories are accurately recorded for future reflection, but also helps us to evaluate emotions that we experienced in certain situations. From there, we can look for patterns experienced in different areas of life and core wounds that may need to be addressed.

- **Meditation.** Meditation is a wonderful tool that can be an aid to objectively reflect upon ourselves. It helps clear out biases and brings us back to the present. It is incredibly powerful and significantly improves our ability to find contradictory proof throughout the day.

- **Open Communication.** Discuss what you felt throughout the day with your friends, partners, or family. By doing this, you have a sounding board to help you assess the validity of the stories you tell yourself. For example, if you interpreted a friend's reaction in one way, your partner may be able to give you a new way to look at the situation. Talking through challenges with someone who can be open and unbiased often helps to remove the untrue stories we are telling ourselves.

There are a variety of ways to implement certain aspects of CBT in our daily lives, but it is essential to step back and do a deep dive when you feel strongly triggered about something. Generally, the more meaning assigned to a situation and the more pain caused by it, the deeper the trigger and the more important it is to address. By following these steps, fundamental change can be seen in all areas of your life.

Chapter 5

FOCUSING ON THE HERE AND NOW

In this chapter we will explore the relationship between traditional Emotion-Focused Therapy (EFT) and the additional practices that I have empirically found helpful in thousands of case studies. We will explore the relationship between your attachment style, the core subconscious wounds within that attachment, and the traditional techniques practiced in EFT.

Emotion-Focused Therapy is a technique used to diffuse emotional distress. Developed by Gary Craig in the late 1990s, it pulls from a variety of therapeutic tools such as neurolinguistic programming and Thought Field Therapy. It focuses on the notion that emotions are intended to be used as a guide and that dismissing them can cause long-term psychological harm.

EFT focuses on three primary concepts:

1. How emotions are produced

2. How emotions affect human functionality

3. How emotions are related to thought and behavior

Within the core concepts, EFT examines how emotions are experienced physically, affect physiological functions, influence thinking, and impact behavior. By using EFT, an individual can better understand their emotions and remove themselves from behaving emotionally rather than logically. By expanding on traditional EFT teachings and partnering them with attachment theory, you can better navigate conflicts and understand what your emotions are trying to tell you.

The practices outlined in this chapter are excellent for any attachment style; however, they will be especially helpful for the Anxious Attachment, the Fearful-Avoidant, and the Dismissive-Avoidant. Since each of these attachment styles has unmet subconscious needs that are easily triggered, an approach that combines the subconscious and EFT will help resolve disputes. Moreover, since competing needs are inevitable in any relationship, the approach outlined in this chapter will help guide us back to more positively oriented practices.

Diving into Your Emotions

To illustrate how EFT works, how to expand upon its traditional teachings, and how to work through attachment theory in conjunction with EFT, imagine that a conflict arises between two sisters. The younger sister, Emily, has an Anxious Attachment. The older sister, Julie, is a Dismissive-Avoidant. They are arguing over who gets to take the family car for the weekend. Emily wants to borrow it to go to a friend's cottage. Julie wants to use it to go into the city and visit her significant other. Remember that since they have different attachment styles, each of their core wounds is being projected onto the argument through the form of different beliefs or stories about the circumstances. Emily fears that, without committing time and energy into her friendships, she risks losing her friends. Julie has recently gotten into an argument with her partner and has taken space over the last few days to process the argument. Julie feels as though if she doesn't go into the city to resolve things, her relationship could be in trouble.

Different beliefs will also be projected onto their argument. Julie will withdraw from Emily when they argue in order to process her emotions. Emily will fear that she is losing her emotional connection with her sister and will attempt to talk things through immediately afterward. Now that the argument between the two sisters is outlined and their core wounds and beliefs are illustrated, we can explore what EFT would reveal about the circumstances and in which ways we can expand on traditional EFT theory.

Identify What Feelings Were Present in the Conflict

In previous chapters, we outlined the importance of taking a moment to witness and identify the feelings that arise in conflict. This simple technique reactivates the neocortex and shifts our brains back into a logical state. According to traditional EFT, an individual would question how their emotions were produced, what physical reaction these caused, and how the emotions could influence future behavior.

Take a moment to recognize in which areas you are feeling your emotions in your body. If you are angry, maybe you feel tenseness in your fists. If you are nervous or anxious, maybe there is a pit in your stomach. Identify all the feelings that are present. The simple act of witnessing and inquiring will move you into a reflective state and out of a reactive state.

In the case of Emily and Julie, each sister would feel different things in different areas due to their attachment styles. Emily would likely feel fearful and clingy toward Julie after the initial argument and may feel it in her stomach or chest. Julie would, as a Dismissive-Avoidant, feel withdrawn and may feel frustration in her extremities as a result of her flight response. If both sisters were to take a moment to consider their emotions and where they are feeling them, they will shift in their brains into the cortex and neocortex and be better prepared to resolve the conflict.

Ultimately, the first step in traditional EFT is to dive into your emotions. Witness them so that you can identify them and move to a more logical perspective. The next step is to identify what triggers these emotions. Ask yourself: *Why are these emotions arising?* However, at this point I recommend veering away from conventional EFT teachings. Instead ask yourself: *What subconscious core wounds created these triggers?*

For example, Julie will notice that she has withdrawn because she is triggered by emotional connection. Julie must then look at the core wound that triggers the withdrawal. In the case of the Dismissive-Avoidant, it is because of the significant emotional neglect they experienced as a child and their belief that self-reliance is the only way to self-preserve.

Identify What Triggers Were Fired

How do you identify which of your triggers were activated? You must identify which negative core belief you *perceive* was validated.

Ask yourself:

- *What do I believe this conflict means?*

- *What am I afraid will happen?*

I have worked with thousands of clients that have been able to distill their perceptions down to painful core beliefs by taking the first step of asking such foundational questions. To help illustrate how these questions can reveal core wounds, consider the argument between the two sisters. Regarding using the car, Emily would ask: "What am I afraid will happen?"

The answer for the Anxious Attachment may be: "My friends will leave me because I am not good enough." In relation to her sister, her answer may be: "I will lose an emotional connection with my sister because of this argument." As you can see, our perceptions are shaped by our core wounds or beliefs. These perceptions are projected onto arguments and create meaning for individuals that may not be understood or obvious to the person on the other side of the conflict. Without understanding core beliefs and how they are triggered, communication in relationships becomes very difficult.

For Julie, the answer to "What do I believe this conflict means?" would likely be: "My sister does not understand that my romantic relationship is in turmoil, and that I am expressing this caused pain. Vulnerability always results in pain." The conflict about the car triggered their core wounds in both their sisterly relationship and the relationships that are affected by using the car. Without asking yourself these two key questions, the triggers that are being activated will not be revealed, and the conflict will be significantly more painful.

Evaluate Your Level of Emotion

At this stage, it is important to evaluate your emotional charge. Once you've witnessed your emotions and identified the underlying trigger that is contributing to your pain, ask yourself: *On a scale from 1 to 10, 10 being most negative, how are my feelings?* In traditional EFT, an individual would be encouraged to observe their emotions for a period while they process them and calm down. Physiologically, their brain would shift back into higher processes, and their reptilian brain would deactivate. By also identifying the core subconscious wound that is present, you can find proof of the opposite to begin lessening the emotional charge associated with said trigger. For example, Emily could remind herself of all the times that, despite her arguments with Julie, they made up once Julie had the opportunity to process her feelings. Julie could also find proof of the opposite by remembering every time that Emily supported her when she *did* share her feelings.

By examining the root cause of the situational pain from a reflective standpoint rather than a reactive standpoint, both sisters would gain the ability to communicate with one another more clearly about what they need. Once they are in a positively oriented headspace, they can find a solution together. In this case, it may be that Julie drops Emily off at the cottage prior to seeing her partner in the city.

- At this point, what would be the emotional charge on the conflict for each of the sisters?

- If you were in a similar conflict, what would you feel out of 10 now?

Keep in mind that it is important to express your feelings when you are feeling approximately 5 out of 10 or less on an emotional scale, since you're likely more disidentified from your emotions. At a 6 or above, expression may not be conducive to finding a solution because you are still in a reactive headspace. You are still highly emotional, and your judgment will be clouded.

Expressing Your Emotions

Research into the subconscious mind has discovered that, for roughly the first seven years of life, the brain is in an almost hypnotic state. In the years of early childhood, the brain produces mostly alpha and theta brainwaves while awake—the same brain waves produced under hypnosis.

As a result, in childhood we are essentially human sponges for information. The young mind has enormous learning capacity and is deeply impacted by many aspects of its environment. During this period, we are having many critical experiences that shape our world view and perception of life.

One of these critical sets of experiences is what we learn about conflict. Conflict is a part of the human experience. It is inevitable and is often a beautiful opportunity for growth when handled appropriately. Yet our earliest experiences of conflict are often quite painful.

Imagine Liam, a five-year-old who is full of life and curiosity. One day, Liam is playing outside in his front yard and has the idea to go ask his neighbor across the street to play with him. Liam is inspired by this exciting notion and jumps up to go running across the street. He isn't thinking about cars passing, and fear is completely absent from his mind.

Just as Liam goes to run across the street his mother yanks him backwards by his shirt and yells at him. His mother was terrified while watching him attempt to run across the street without looking for cars and was petrified by the thought that, if she wasn't there to stop him, something awful could have happened.

Liam, on the other hand, feels extreme disappointment and frustration toward his mother. One moment he was having the time of his life, and the next he was being yelled at and pulled around aggressively. He feels that she doesn't understand his innocence. He didn't mean to do anything wrong. He is helpless to explain himself, and when he tries to assert himself to his mother, she is not listening. Liam experiences shame, sadness, and helplessness in this moment.

This is one example of many of Liam's experiences in childhood, as it is for most individuals growing up. Parents discipline their kids because they are trying to keep them safe, but it often doesn't go well. Often the pain and worry of the parent gets lost in translation and seems harsh, punishing, or shaming to the child.

Two key factors are responsible for programming the subconscious: repetition and emotion.

As a result, our very suggestible subconscious minds tend to associate conflict with shame, helplessness, sadness, feeling misunderstood, and other painful feelings. The more times an experience is repeated, the deeper our programming will become. The more emotional an experience is, the more intense the programming will also become. These two factors create a challenging dynamic, as most of our childhood is spent in the socialization process.

How many times do you think Liam experienced moments like that with his mother? He experienced being reprimanded when he wanted to walk down the stairs before he was old enough. He experienced punishment when he tried to put his hands on the stove when it was hot. Almost every day throughout childhood Liam was on the receiving end of some sort of reprimand or anger.

This is how most individuals grew up, which means most of the subconscious associations about conflict are quite painful. In Liam's adult life, he is likely to still be carrying many of these same programs unless he has done extensive work to overcome them. Liam's mind says conflict equals punishment and shaming.

Now let's fast-forward twenty years. Liam is now in a long-term relationship with his first girlfriend, Faith. Liam has a Dismissive-Avoidant attachment style, while his girlfriend Faith is Anxious.

One evening Liam forgets to call Faith back on his way home from work. He had a tough day at his new job and was preoccupied in his mind. When he arrives home, Faith is distressed. She expresses anxiety and frustration toward Liam for not contacting her. Immediately, Liam is experiencing Faith's emotions along with all the stored associations in his own subconscious. Rather than being able to be present and listen to Faith's feelings, his mind feels attacked and jumps at the need to protect and defend himself.

Liam raises his voice back at Faith. He tells her to leave him alone and that he had a stressful day. He isn't able to validate her emotions and judges her for getting upset with him. He feels like she's shaming him and experiences resentment, sadness, helplessness. He also feels gravely misunderstood.

Liam's emotional response in this moment is a combination of emotions from the situation with Faith, along with stored emotional associations rising from the past. The subconscious mind stores all memories and, as we know, the emotional associations are still alive within those memories, waiting to surface.

Liam and Faith both struggle to communicate, and it makes sense. They are both experiencing unresolved triggers that have been stored subconsciously.

- How can they bypass this challenge?

- How can they communicate with one another without triggering each other along the way?

First and foremost, it is important to recognize another important reason that arguments with our loved ones can cause so much pain. Most of us think that we are arguing about being right versus being wrong. The truth is, we are almost always arguing about being seen, heard, and understood by our loved ones. It is painful to feel as though someone you love does not understand you in the heat of the moment. It often feels like we are disconnected, and usually that is what hurts more than anything else.

This is where a beautiful first step comes in. It is possible to validate a person's feelings without validating their behavior. If Liam used this tool, he might say to Faith, "Hi, honey. I can see that you're hurting right now, and I'm sorry for that. However, I don't like the way you are expressing it, and I would be able to listen better if you could change your approach to become gentler."

Although this might seem like a small trick, it works wonders. The impact of being able to validate a loved one's emotions in the heat of the moment is profound. It completely removes the helplessness, feelings of being misunderstood, and feeling shamed. More importantly, it prevents the defense mechanism from being tripped due to the stored subconscious associations around conflict. As a result, the individual on the receiving end of this statement is likely to be calmed down instead of fired up.

If Faith used the proper tools to communicate with Liam, she would also express her anxiety and frustration in a more appropriate way. As discussed in the CBT section of this book, most of the pain we experience in a situation is based on the subjective meaning we give to a situation as opposed to the objective content of the experience itself. This is why you might see Faith react differently if a friend forgot to call her than if Liam forgot to call her back.

As Faith is waiting for Liam to arrive home and feeling the need to unload her emotions onto him, it is important for her to identify this meaning. It is then important for her to express that she is upset because of her interpretation of the situation, and to share from that perspective.

She might say, "Liam, I know you had a long day at work, but when you didn't call me back I interpreted that to mean that you don't care about me, and it really hurt. I need you to be more conscious about this in the future and maybe set a reminder on your phone."

Faith is following these steps:

1. Identify the meaning you give to a situation.

2. Express using the following:

   "When _____ (insert
   the situation) happened, I interpreted it to mean
   _____ (insert the
   meaning you gave to it), and I felt _____
   _____ (insert the emotion
   you experienced)."

3. Identify what you need from your loved one and
   the strategy they can use to meet that need better.

4. Express using the following:

   "I need you to _____
   (insert what you need). You can do this by
   _____ (insert
   the "how"/strategy they can use)."

This set of steps does four crucial things:

1. Because it expresses what Faith's experience and
   interpretation are, it lowers the likelihood of Liam
   getting triggered. This depersonalization makes it
   highly unlikely that Liam's need to protect himself
   and his negative associations with conflict will
   be triggered.

2. It allows Faith to express from a place of vulnerability. She is most likely to be heard when she is
   vulnerable, because human beings are naturally
   open and receptive to vulnerability. Just think of
   the way you naturally look at a puppy or a baby.
   Expressing from vulnerability also opens the
   human capacity to be present.

3. Faith offers a solution to Liam. It is so easy to fall into the trap of expressing hurt without expressing a way that a loved one can make that hurt better. This often leaves the problem only partially solved, as sometimes the need for resolution can be ambiguous.

4. Faith describes the "how" for Liam. It is common for couples to try to resolve challenges by projecting what they would need onto their partner and attempting to do that instead.

Let's pretend that Faith said to Liam that she needed to feel supported by him. Maybe Liam feels supported by Faith when she cooks him a meal. So, the day after an argument, he tries to do that for her to be supportive. When Faith expressed the need for support, she secretly wanted Liam to compliment her and make her feel validated through words. She appreciates the meal but feels as though Liam "didn't try hard enough."

It is extremely common for couples to have different interpretations about how their needs can be met by one another. This is why the "how" is so important in the first step. Although it would be nice if Faith and Liam could read each other's minds, that just isn't how it works.

These four steps should be your gold standard for communication. Take some time to practice them. Think of three or four different times you felt frustrated in conflict and put them through these steps. Once you feel as though you know the steps like the back of your hand, practice applying them to challenging situations in your life.

Active listening is also an important part of resolving conflict, so remember to allow space for your partner to respectfully communicate to you as well.

Exploring Productive Ways to Respond: Diving Deeper

EFT falls into three phases:

1. Assess and de-escalate

2. Change events

3. Consolidate change

The first phase focuses on witnessing and uncovering the initial emotional trigger. Then, one must focus on how to effectively communicate this core wound or trigger. Last, communication must be effectively received for long-lasting change.

Individuals consistently are caught up in how their emotions make them feel, and they often forget how to respond to others' emotions. An essential concept to remember from the previous section is that people are very rarely arguing about being right or wrong; they're more often arguing about being seen and heard. People feel so much pain in intense conflict with those they care about because, when someone has a different perspective, our subconscious perceives it as our feelings being treated as invalid. This ultimately feeds conflict.

So, begin by validating the emotions of the person who is expressing them to you. However, keep in mind that there is a significant difference between validating *emotions* and validating *behavior*. For example, if Emily were to get angry in the argument and storm out of the room, her conduct would be hurtful and unproductive. To validate Emily's emotions but not her behavior, Julie should say to Emily: "I see that you're hurt, which has led to an outburst of emotion. I would like to hear more about why you feel this way, but you cannot behave in such an explosive manner." This is an extreme example of how emotions can be validated, while actions are not.

Reframing the Problem

To help validate the emotions of a partner or family member at a time where your personal emotions are running high, begin by reframing the problem. This practice is also known as *cognitive reframing*. Cognitive reframing is the process of actively or voluntarily shifting your perspective to view an issue or situation from a more objective space.

According to management coach Carter McNamara, there are multiple ways in which this can be done. A few examples include shifting from passive to active and shifting from others to oneself. The former is an action-oriented approach that empowers the individual attempting to reframe the situation. For example, Emily can reframe her thinking from "I will lose my emotional connection with Julie if we do not resolve this conflict immediately" to "What does Julie need right now to feel as though we can make up? What do I need right now? What steps can I take to find a compromise?"

The latter reframing approach involves viewing yourself from another perspective entirely. For example, Julie can reframe her perspective from "Emily does not support me" to "What can I do right now to support myself?" By partaking in cognitive reframing, both sisters will be better equipped to reflect on how they are feeling and how they can communicate these needs to their sibling. They will also be better prepared to hear their sibling's feelings and respond to them in a constructive manner. It is also helpful if a verbal shift occurs. Use connective language such as "together," "we," and "us" so that the conscious mind shifts out of a space of feeling defensive.

Acceptance

Next, focus on acceptance.

- *In what ways do you need acceptance from the person you are experiencing conflict with?*

- *In what ways can you accept them?*

To understand how to reach a compromise and ultimately acceptance, start with what attachment style you and the other person involved in this situation have.

To illustrate what this can look like, recall Julie and Emily. Transparency in the case of an Anxious Attachment is essential. Since they tend to be people-pleasing, it is imperative that they do not sacrifice their needs and that they communicate them properly. If not, the Anxious individual will begin to harbor resentment. For Emily, this means communicating to Julie that she needs to talk things through because she feels as though she is at risk of losing her emotional connection to her sister.

However, she must also accept that Julie may need a bit more time than she does to talk through the conflict. Julie, on the other hand, must communicate that she needs time to process her emotions and accept that she may have to do this more quickly to be considerate of how Emily feels. Ultimately, this means both sisters express how they are triggered and that they must be accepting and considerate of both their own needs and their sibling's.

It is important to also create a clear, coherent strategy for the needs that have been expressed and accepted. Since perceptions for every individual are uniquely shaped over time, saying "I need support" may mean different things to different people. Therefore, Emily must communicate to Julie that in the future she needs to feel like she has an emotional connection to her sister, which may include Julie lending her the family car when she is concerned about her friendships. It also may include acts like getting dinner together to discuss their lives and talking more frequently.

On the days they are not together, Julie should communicate to Emily that she needs time alone to read and pursue the things she enjoys independently. In the end, the goal is to have both parties hear each other's feelings, validate each other's and their own feelings, and express themselves in a way that allows them to compromise and set boundaries within which they can operate.

TIP

EFT can be implemented in daily life in a variety of ways. The following are some examples of ways that you can practice traditional EFT and the additional subconscious work I have developed.

- **Cognitive Reframing**. Practice cognitive reframing during everyday activities. If, for example, you walk into a room and think: *No one here likes me*, reframe it in a *oneself* manner—ask yourself: *What do I like about myself?* This shifts you into an observational space, reduces the emotional charge of the situation, and helps to put you into a positive headspace.
- **Write It Down**. As mentioned in previous chapters, writing down the process by which you sublimate conflict helps you process it more effectively. Physically write down the triggers you experience and how you resolve them. This will help work through conflict more easily while reprogramming your subconscious through repetition and emotion.

WRAP-UP

To conclude Julie and Emily's story, imagine that they followed all of the steps described in this chapter. When Emily got mad at Julie and stormed out of the room, she paused and witnessed her emotions—where they are in her body—and labeled what she was feeling. Then, she asked herself: "What am I afraid will happen here?" Her response was: "That I will lose the emotional connection with my sister and friends." This led her to realize that she felt this way because her core wound, consistent with her Anxious attachment style, was triggered: the fear of abandonment because of her inconsistent parenting.

Then, she would evaluate her emotional level by recognizing the trigger and witnessing it, and she will feel less pain associated with the situation because she is better prepared to navigate it. By expressing this to Julie, she will be prepared to find a compromise for the situation at hand. Given Julie follows the same approach, both sisters will have communicated what they are feeling and why they are feeling it, and they therefore will both be more empathetic toward the other's circumstances and more willing to find a solution—instead of yelling and not talking to each other.

By combining EFT and attachment theory and using the results-oriented techniques I have distilled, Julie and Emily will come to a solution that is better for themselves and their relationships. Now, apply these steps to a conflict you are experiencing to create effective change.

Chapter 6

CULTIVATING WISDOM THROUGH MINDFULNESS AND RAIN

In this chapter, we will explore the relationship between attachment styles and a mindfulness technique called RAIN. RAIN helps create a foundation upon which the subconscious can be explored. Recall from previous chapters that mindfulness is the act of removing yourself from an emotionally reactive state to a witnessing state. Through the act of self-observation, a more logical and constructive solution can be found during conflict.

Moreover, it provides the unique opportunity to work through limiting subconscious beliefs as they arise. By combining the underlying core wounds expressed in attachment style schema with the ability to connect with your internal self through RAIN, a more Secure attachment style can eventually be achieved.

This process will help ease conflict in relationships of any kind and will enable you to better understand how emotions relate to subconscious beliefs and the behaviors that are elicited as a response. To better understand the information in this chapter, an anecdotal story about two best friends will be used. Their names are Chris and Suneel. Chris is an Anxious Attachment and Suneel is a Fearful-Avoidant. While living together, conflict arises over Suneel's messiness.

RAIN techniques will be used to work through this conflict, and both men's underlying core wounds will be identified. By combining these two theories in the way that I outline, you will have yet another toolset to use to come to the best possible solution when dealing with conflict.

RAIN

As with any therapeutic technique mentioned in this book, RAIN is effective for individuals looking to improve themselves. Ultimately, RAIN will work the best in conflict between different attachment styles. However, it can also be used to resolve any instance in which needs are unmet. Moreover, it is useful to help reflect on prior experiences and to bring mindfulness into everyday life.

Research from Dr. Meera Joshi has shown that when someone practices mindfulness there is a change in the production of neurochemicals that alter mood. Moreover, Magnetic Resonance Imaging (MRI) has shown that certain areas of the brain may even change in size over time in response to mindfulness practices. The amygdala, which is responsible for emotional regulation—most famously, creating stress—shows a decrease in size. The prefrontal cortex, responsible for problem solving among other things, has been shown to become thicker after continual mindfulness practices. Last, according to Dr. Joshi, the hippocampus, which is responsible for memory and learning, has also shown similar thickening.

In summary, mindfulness can help you better respond to your environment and become more attuned with your internal dialogue, and it can even shape your brain in ways that better prepare you for the challenges life presents.

Basics of RAIN

RAIN is an acronym for a four-step process that helps to induce mindfulness:

- Recognize—recognize what is happening

- Allow—allow life to be just as it is

- Investigate—investigate with kindness

- Non-identification

Developed by Buddhist teachers and coined by RAIN by meditation instructor Michele McDonald, RAIN is intended to create self-compassion and recondition internal resistance. After a rare-degenerative-disease diagnosis, Tara Brach looked to combine Western medicine and Buddhism as a coping mechanism for those in emotional distress.

Recognize What Is Happening

The first step calls for you to recognize what is happening. This, in a similar manner to EFT, ACT, and CBT, calls for the witnessing of your emotions. From a RAIN perspective, recognizing what is happening grounds one in the moment and moves one into a positively oriented space rather than a reactive space.

Moreover, extremely emotional circumstances can be confusing. By taking a moment to question what emotions are present, individuals can more easily navigate through what unmet needs they have and what solution may be the best for every party involved in a conflict.

To help illustrate the RAIN technique, consider our two friends who are in a fight: Suneel and Chris. Suneel is a Fearful-Avoidant, and Chris is an Anxious Attachment. They live together, and Chris is upset with Suneel because he doesn't clean up after himself. When Chris confronts Suneel, Suneel is initially very receptive. Although he gets frustrated, he promises to make a change. However, as weeks go by, Suneel doesn't make a tangible change. He withdraws from Chris, and Chris begins to fear that he has upset Suneel and negatively impacted their friendship. So, when he confronts Suneel again, Suneel gets frustrated and says that Chris is being overbearing.

Both of these responses—Suneel's unpredictable emotional responses and Chris's need to resolve conflict—are classic, given their attachment styles. However, they must each take a moment to recognize what is happening. By doing this, they will be more receptive to the feedback of the other person and will be more likely to identify that their responses are in accordance with their core wounds.

Suneel must ask himself: "What am I feeling right now?" In this instance, for a Fearful-Avoidant, he would likely feel hurt by Chris's criticism since it triggers his core wound of feeling that relationships result in pain and causes him to become torn between showing up emotionally for his friend and withdrawing from the vulnerability. Superficially, Chris's reaction would appear to Suneel as anger and confusion. Chris, on the other hand, would feel anxious about his friend's withdrawal and intense emotional response.

Since Chris has an Anxious Attachment, he would experience the core trigger of feeling excluded or alone. Superficially, this would lead to a sense of unease, frustration, and vulnerability. The act of recognizing that he is experiencing an emotional response is Chris's first step to identifying what the reaction is trying to tell him.

The second phase of recognition is realizing what physiological response is also occurring. Chris may realize he is feeling uneasy and respond physiologically by being jittery or tensing. Keep in mind that it is essential to recognize what is happening without being judgmental toward yourself. Suneel, for example, should not be upset with himself for withdrawing, because he has a core childhood wound that has not yet been addressed. Instead, he should turn inward and focus on the present moment. This will help him sort his preconceived ideas and move past outdated beliefs to better understand the reality of the situation at hand.

In other words, Chris has a preconceived subconscious belief that he will be abandoned. This is what causes his anxiety to arise under these circumstances. By taking a moment to focus on the present, he will be able to more clearly navigate through the outdated childhood belief that everyone will abandon him just like his parents did emotionally.

RAIN provides a unique opportunity to further delve into your attachment style and shift it into a more Secure space. By using these mindfulness techniques, you'll be able to understand your core wounds and create longer-lasting change through their routine application.

Allow Life to Be Just as It Is

The second step in RAIN is allowing life to be just as it is. Once you recognize that you are feeling something, allow it to happen. Often, people feel a sense of aversion to strong waves of emotion. Unpleasant feelings such as frustration, anger, or nervousness are often met with a strong urge to quickly correct the situation. However, if you just let yourself feel the emotions that arise in certain circumstances, you become grounded in that moment and consciously open to understanding what your emotions are telling you.

Some who partake of RAIN therapy offer words of encouragement to themselves throughout this process, for example, when faced with anxiety, speaking the word "yes." This is done multiple times until the feelings are truly allowed to exist in the present as they are. This removes resistance, emotional repression, and negative subconscious programming. By allowing life to be just as it is, your emotional response will stay surfaced in the present to be investigated in the next step of the RAIN process.

The process of allowing is also known to some as "softening." By accepting that the emotion is occurring, rather than experiencing it *and* resisting it, the cumulative effect will be "softened." Softening is a unique by-product of practicing RAIN. By dulling the emotional blow of a painful situation, an individual can navigate their feelings more seamlessly.

They will also be more likely to practice RAIN in the future, as their subconscious will work to recall these techniques in favor of protecting itself from uncomfortable feelings. Allowing life to just be as it is is a unique stage in RAIN as it is derived from a variety of historical psychological practices.

This stage of RAIN is built upon the foundation of centuries of psychological research. The origins of modern psychology can be found in 1879, when a German scientist by the name of Wilhelm Wundt founded the first known psychological institution. This institution physically marked the separation of psychology from the fields of biology and philosophy. However, philosophical investigation into the human mind and its behavior can be traced back to ancient Egypt, Greece, India, and China.

In recent studies by David Barlow and Steven Hayes, many adulthood psychological issues were found to be rooted in the habit of emotional avoidance. Although emotional avoidance eases feelings of unpleasantness in the short-term, it can go as far as to inhibit ambitions, create chaos in relationships, and limit the individual's ability to meet life's challenges.

> *By avoiding feelings such as anxiety, one will become hypervigilant to scenarios where this anxiety may arise.*

Moreover, emotional avoidance is often futile. It essentially creates a self-fulfilling prophecy where anxiety arises *about* anxiety. To make the situation even worse, anticipatory anxiety can then arise, which tends to be even more challenging to cope with than the event that may bring about anxiety itself. As you can see, without the use of proper emotional coping mechanisms, emotional avoidance can create serious turmoil in an individual's life.

This is why allowing is imperative. It softens the emotions felt and it prevents emotional repression. To demonstrate this stage of RAIN, recall Chris and Suneel. In the moment that they begin to argue the second time, Suneel should take a moment to accept that he feels frustrated. By doing so, he is less likely to withdraw, as the Fearful-Avoidant does when they feel vulnerable.

Since he is processing and experiencing his emotions in the present moment, he will be better equipped to confront the situation, rather than withdrawing and repressing his emotions. In a way, this will also help reprogram his subconscious core wound of vulnerability resulting in pain. Again, since the subconscious is programmed through repetition and emotion, if Suneel were to take a moment to be mindful of his feelings and avoid withdrawing, he will slowly come to learn subconsciously that vulnerability isn't unsafe.

Consider the same situation for Chris. As an Anxious Attachment, he should accept his anxiety and fearfulness surrounding the relationship. By accepting these feelings, he is less likely to react emotionally and overwhelm Suneel by clinging to him. Like Suneel, Chris can then learn to accept that immediacy isn't a necessity surrounding conflict. He will be able to begin to reprogram his subconscious by realizing, over time, that he will not be abandoned if he does not respond and self-sacrifice. This will also reduce the amount of resentment that Chris feels toward Suneel, as he will be less likely to emotionally abandon his needs to satisfy Suneel's. Over time, the simple act of accepting brings both Chris and Suneel into a better space to deal with their personal issues, as well as their friendship issues.

It is important to remember that the most painful conflicts aren't always about the argument itself—it is about *the meaning that we assign to the argument*. In the case of Chris, he is assigning the idea that Suneel will abandon him because he confronted him about the situation. To Suneel, however, Chris's overbearing nature reinforces the idea that close relationships can be painful. Ultimately, both friends must Allow the emotions that arise in this situation so that they can unroot the underlying beliefs they are projecting onto the argument, and from there, they can move on to the next step of RAIN: investigating.

Investigate with Kindness

The interesting aspect of this RAIN step is that during the investigation of your emotions, you must do it with *kindness*. Since our subconscious mind is wired to protect us, it is often easy to be in denial surrounding our emotions since they are reflective of ourselves—and sometimes that can be uncomfortable. In other words, imagine someone who has done something shameful. It could be, for example, that they cheated on their partner. Often, they will rationalize this action to avoid the shame that they're feeling. They may tell themselves they did it because their partner was unloving or unavailable.

In reality, this is their mind attempting to protect itself from the unpleasant feelings of shame or guilt associated with the situation. Your mind does this in micro-doses throughout the day and does its best to protect you from unpleasant feelings. When considering the attachment styles, you may see this manifested as withdrawal, unpredictability, or clinginess—and more. Therefore, when you are investigating your feelings, do it in an open and loving way. Remember that you are human and we make mistakes. Nobody is perfect and we are all just doing our best.

In the case of the partner who cheated, it is essential for them to accept that they made a mistake and face the residual feelings head-on. This is the only way that a relationship would likely be healed after such an indiscretion and the only way that the individual who trespassed would truly be able to improve themselves.

Keeping the kindness aspect of this RAIN step in mind, we can now move on to what it means to investigate. Investigation is the process of inquiring what your subconscious mind is trying to tell you. In the previous steps, the anecdotal characters had accepted that they were feeling a certain way and allowed it to occur. This is the step that would allow them to understand where these core wounds are coming from. Moreover, it will be indicative of what they both *need* in this situation.

Often, without practicing RAIN, an individual would become emotionally caught up in a situation and make judgments about their external environment. However, such judgments are often inaccurate because, ultimately, everyone has their own attachment style and core wounds, and everyone assigns their own individual meanings to situations.

To begin the investigation process, remember that what you are feeling when you're triggered is everything in the current moment *in addition to all of the past emotions that trigger is associated with*. For example, consider someone with PTSD.

When something in their external present is reminiscent of the original traumatic experiences they've endured, the emotions they'll feel in response to the present event will be significantly stronger due to the past emotions they've stored. Therefore, it is essential to ask yourself questions like: *"What am I believing?"* and *"What emotional response wants the most attention?"* By asking probing questions, you may surface the unmet needs that the situation is calling to satisfy.

Ultimately, your subconscious mind will do nearly everything it its power to meet needs that are seemingly unmet. For example, someone who just got divorced may find themselves watching more romantic comedies because subconsciously their brain is attempting to fill that void. When certain needs are deeply entrenched in the subconscious, actions or behaviors will therefore arise to meet those needs.

For example, consider Suneel and Chris. Chris has a core wound, or void, surrounding reliability in relationships since he was abandoned as a child. When Suneel and Chris argue, Chris's brain craves stability in the relationship—thus, he goes as far as self-sacrificing to meet that need. In this case, it would be ignoring the mess for weeks after their original discussion. His mind believes that it is only by sacrificing his desire for a clean apartment that his relationship with Suneel will continue.

However, this form of self-sacrifice inevitably breeds resentment. As you can see, our brains will elicit certain behaviors as a mechanism to fill unmet needs from our childhood—however, this can often be counterproductive if we don't understand why we are behaving in such ways.

It is essential to investigate during the RAIN process.

- Question what needs you are attempting to meet within the conflict that has arisen.

- How are your emotions guiding you to behave in certain ways?

- What does that tell you about what your core unmet needs are?

Remember that during this process you must be kind to yourself. It can be painful to realize and accept core wounds since they have years or decades of built-up negative emotion retained within them. By being transparent and kind to yourself, you will be more likely to find your true unmet need in the situation.

Once you have discovered your unmet needs, it can be helpful to consider their opposites.

For example, the opposite of feeling abandoned is feeling cherished, adopted, or defended. Once Chris realizes that his core wound surrounds feeling abandoned and discovers that his unmet need is emotional connection, he can look for ways that the opposite emotion has appeared in his life. For example, all the times that Suneel or his other friends have made him feel cherished or defended. The simple act of looking for examples where the opposite emotion of your core wound appears can help neutralize the overall emotional charge in any given circumstance.

In summation, the third step of the RAIN process is to investigate what you are feeling by asking probing questions. These questions will lead you to the core wounds you may have and what unmet needs may exist. This will help you understand your behavior in reaction to those unmet needs and core wounds, and thus can help you identify scenarios where the opposite has occurred. By finding situations that disprove the beliefs surrounding your current circumstances and emotions, the pain experienced from what you are enduring will be lessened greatly.

Non-Identification

The last step of the RAIN process is non-identification. This means disidentifying from who you are emotionally. According to Tara Brach, "your sense of who you are is not fused with or defined by any limited set of emotions, or stories." To Brach, this is a process that arises automatically upon completing the first three steps of RAIN. Once your emotions have been investigated, you reach a stage called "natural awareness." This means that you are freed of the constraints that emotions create, and you can truly observe the situation and yourself from a third-party perspective. Achieving natural awareness does not redefine your sense of self or heal your core wounds, however.

Consider how certain key components of your identity come about: A void is created in childhood because of how you were parented. This, in the case of a Fearful-Avoidant, would be the void of inconsistent emotional connection.

Since we are born with the biological fear of abandonment—as infants we are dependent on our care-givers for survival—a trigger surrounding abandonment is created for the Anxious Attachment. This creates a core wound of believing they will be rejected. Then, the Anxious

Attachment will manifest this subconscious belief in adulthood by being overbearing or self-sacrificing.

A sense of identity can also arise from these core wounds. Since our brains are constantly attempting to meet our needs, the areas where these childhood voids are filled will eventually contribute to our sense of identity. For example, consider this scenario: Chris had parents who were always busy with their work, but were loving and present during the times they did see him. Therefore, he did not learn how to properly self-soothe, and as an infant became anxious when his parents were not present. In his romantic relationships, however, he feels connected, heard, and validated.

Because in this area of his life his core wounds were disproven, he began to identify as a "family man." Although this is a superficial example of how identity relates to your attachment style, your subconscious makes a large contribution to your sense of identity. This last step in RAIN can therefore be further used to move you closer to a Secure attachment style. The essential aspect to consider in this final step is the true importance of removing yourself from a place of reactivity.

By being mindful and disidentifying, we put ourselves in a position to truly achieve the highest expression of ourselves. We cannot be in a state of reactivity and effectively and logically evaluate the situation at hand.

To illustrate how this would occur, we will use the story of Suneel and Chris. Suneel, at this point, has recognized his emotions, accepted that they are happening, and investigated his core wounds. In this last step, he must achieve a state of natural awareness to truly witness the meaning that he is giving to the situation. As a Fearful-Avoidant, his core wounds revolve around feeling unsafe when vulnerable, and, often, a sense of unworthiness.

This is why Chris's criticism hurt him so deeply and caused him to perpetuate unhealthy attachment patterns. Suneel's void pertains to being safe in relationships and not having vulnerability met with pain. One of his core beliefs is that he will be taken advantage of.

When Chris confronts him, without removing himself from his anger and asking why he feels so strongly about such a trivial complaint, he will be unable to trace his emotions back to their root: the pain he associates with relationships. After transcending his anger, he will be examining himself objectively. This is how emotions serve us: They provide us with metaphorical alarm bells to tell us that limiting subconscious beliefs are being activated.

Keep in mind that these techniques also apply to the Dismissive-Avoidant and Secure Attachment. Although the Secure individual has very few core wounds due to the supportive parenting they received, conflicting needs can ultimately result in argument. If you are a Secure individual, practice each step of the RAIN process to put yourself in the best possible space to resolve conflict.

The RAIN process for the Dismissive-Avoidant, however, is slightly more complicated than that of the Secure individual. The Dismissive-Avoidant suffered emotional neglect as a child. Therefore, their core wounds involve feeling unsafe.

Their core beliefs are often that they are defective because they were not given the attention they desired when they were young. If Chris were a Dismissive-Avoidant:

- He would first recognize that he is having an emotional response to the conflict with Suneel.

- Then, he would have to allow himself to feel what this response is. He may verbally say "yes" to reaffirm that he is allowed to feel what he is feeling.

- Then, he must investigate with kindness: *"What am I believing?"*

In this case, he may believe that Chris is criticizing him because he is defective—an affirmation of his negative and outdated subconscious beliefs. He can then trace this back to his core wound: "Relationships are unsafe, and I must solely rely on myself."

As you can see, this is an unhealthy and untrue belief that, without the first three steps of RAIN, would not have been addressed. Then, by non-identifying he can truly understand that the emotions that exist in this situation are there to guide him to a better version of himself. From this point, he would be equipped to look for proof of the opposite and begin to reprogram his subconscious.

In conclusion, RAIN is a mindfulness technique that can be paired with my empirical findings on the subconscious mind and attachment styles to shift ourselves into a more Secure Attachment space. It is one of many techniques that is incredibly useful to guide us to a more objective viewpoint that will allow self-exploration.

As mentioned in previous chapters, there are a variety of ways to effectively implement mindfulness in your day. Below are some easy ways to try:

- **Meditation.** As with other forms of therapy, meditation is an incredible way to practice mindfulness. It provides you with a quiet, physiologically primed opportunity to look inwards and observe your emotions objectively.

- **Reflection.** Periodically checking in on yourself throughout the day, inquiring about what thoughts you have, and reflecting on the emotions that were produced by them, is a great way to ground yourself in the present. It also helps to keep in check the automatic thoughts that were referenced in the CBT chapter and will take you off of autopilot.

- **Exercise.** Among the other physical benefits that exercising has, it also provides you with an uninterrupted opportunity to check in with yourself—both physically and emotionally. Going for a run on a quiet path or a stroll in your neighborhood can give you the space you need to reach a natural-awareness state.

- **Communication**. All self-reflection does not necessarily have to be practiced alone. If you are new to being mindful, or would like to help introduce RAIN to others, talk through a situation together and help discover yourselves concurrently. Ensure that the environment is open, positive, and honest. It is essential that during this process you are validating to one another.

Ultimately, there is room to be mindful during any situation—especially in those where tensions may be running high, or when you have a quiet opportunity for self-reflection. Remember that, by working on yourself, you can both improve your personal well-being and the well-being of your relationships and others around you.

WRAP-UP

By using RAIN and taking the opportunity to look at our perceptions and beliefs intrinsically, outdated wounds can be uprooted and reprogrammed. At this point we can re-examine the conflict between Suneel and Chris.

Once Suneel realized his core beliefs as a Fearful-Avoidant were being triggered, he looked for proof of the opposite. This allowed him to recognize all of the times that he was safe to express himself and helped him neutralize the negative feelings he had in regards to Chris's confrontation. From there, he was less emotional and did not take Chris's request personally.

Suneel realized that his busy schedule conflicted with his ability to tidy, and that he should prioritize organization at home. The situation no longer subconsciously meant to Suneel that he was unworthy and that interaction results in pain. Conversely, Chris learned that he will not be abandoned for expressing his needs.

Chris was able to communicate that Suneel's withdrawal was painful for him because of his childhood experiences, and he realized he could ask gently for Suneel to be aware of his reactions in the future. Moreover, he did not self-sacrifice, and worked to compromise with Suneel on a cleaning schedule.

Ultimately, RAIN provided both Suneel and Chris with the tools to neutralize their emotional triggers in this situation. Imagine how significantly your life would change if you were to practice this in every area of your life. The cumulative effect of being aware of your attachment style, core wounds, and beliefs and having the tools to address them can create enormous positive change in your life.

REFERENCES

Ackerman, Courtney. "Emotion Focused Therapy: Understanding Emotions to Improve Relationships." *Positive
Psychology*. June 19, 2019. positivepsychology.com
/emotion-focused-therapy.

Beckwith, Helen. "What Is Attachment Theory Used For?"
The Association for Child and Adolescent Mental Health.
May 17, 2018. acamh.org/blog/attachment-theory
-applications.

Boundless.com. "Introduction to Psychology." Lumen Learning. Accessed October 10, 2019. courses.lumenlearning
.com/boundless-psychology/chapter/introduction-to
-the-field-of-psychology.

Brach, Tara. "Working with Difficulties: The Blessing of
RAIN." 2013. tarabrach.com/articles-interviews/rain
-workingwithdifficulties.

Bretherton, Inge. "The Origins of Attachment Theory."
Developmental Psychology. 1992. psychology.sunysb
.edu/attachment/online/inge_origins.pdf.

Bydlowska, Jowita. "Drugs, Guilt and Recovery with Dr. Gabor
Maté: A Therapy Session Disguised as Q&A." *Hazlitt*.
August 9, 2014. hazlitt.net/feature/drugs-guilt-and
-recovery-dr-gabor-mate-therapy-session-disguised-qa.

CDC. "Early Brain Development and Health." Centers for
Disease Control and Prevention. February 6, 2019.
cdc.gov/ncbddd/childdevelopment/early-brain
-development.html.

Center on the Developing Child. "Toxic Stress." Harvard
University. Accessed October 1, 2019. https://
developingchild.harvard.edu/science/key-concepts
/toxic-stress/.

Chapman, Gary. "Discover Your Love Language." Accessed
October 3, 2019. 5lovelanguages.com.

Craig, Gary, and Tina Craig. "Welcome to The Gold Standard
(Official) EFT Tapping Tutorial." 1995. emofree.com/eft
-tutorial/eft-tapping-tutorial.html.

GoodTherapy. "Are Attachment Styles Specific to Relationships?" *GoodTherapy Therapy Blog*. December 7, 2012.
goodtherapy.org/blog/are-attachment-styles-specific
-to-relationships.

GoodTherapy. "Emotion-Focused Therapy." *GoodTherapy
Therapy Blog*. June 22, 2019. goodtherapy.org/learn
-about-therapy/types/emotion-focused-therapy.

Hayes, Steven. "Acceptance and Commitment Therapy
(ACT)." Association for Contextual Behavioral Science.
Accessed October 3, 2019. contextualscience.org/act.

Joshi, Meera. "How Does Mindfulness Affect the Brain?
[Video]." Bupa UK. November 10, 2017. bupa.co.uk
/newsroom/ourviews/mindfulness-my-brain.

Kassam, Karim S., Amanda R. Markey, Vladimir L. Cherkassky,
George Loewenstein, and Marcel Adam Just. "Identifying
Emotions on the Basis of Neural Activation." *PLoS ONE*
(forthcoming). Accessed October 3, 2019. cmu.edu
/dietrich/sds/docs/loewenstein/EmotionNeuralAct.pdf.

Lanese, Nicoletta. "Fight or Flight: The Sympathetic Nervous System." *Live Science*. May 9, 2019. livescience
.com/65446-sympathetic-nervous-system.html.

Lenneville, Emily. "What Physiological Changes Can Explain
the Honeymoon Phase of a Relationship?" *Scientific
American*. September 1, 2013. scientificamerican.com
/article/what-physiological-changes-can-explain
-honeymoon-phase-relationship.

Lipton, Bruce. "Epigenetics." Accessed October 3, 2019.
brucelipton.com/resource/article/epigenetics.

Marcus, Joshua. "Enmeshment: How To Unmesh From Your Dysfunctional Family." *ThriveTalk*. June 19, 2019. thrivetalk.com/enmeshment.

McGill University. "The Evolutionary Layers of the Human Brain." Accessed October 3, 2019. thebrain.mcgill.ca /flash/d/d_05/d_05_cr/d_05_cr_her/d_05_cr_her .html.

McLeod, Saul. "Wilhelm Wundt." *Simply Psychology*. 2008. simplypsychology.org/wundt.html.

McNamara, Carter. "Basic Guidelines to Reframing—to Seeing Things Differently." Coaching and Action Learning. February 2, 2012. managementhelp.org/blogs /personal-and-professional-coaching/2012/02/02/basic -guidelines-to-reframing-to-seeing-things-differently.

Mikulincer, Mario, and Phillip R. Shaver. "The Attachment Behavioral System In Adulthood: Activation, Psycho-dynamics, And Interpersonal Processes." *Advances in Experimental Social Psychology* 35 (2003): 53–152. doi.org/10.1016/S0065-2601(03)01002-5.

Newman, Louise, Carmel Sivaratnam, and Angela Komiti. "Attachment and Early Brain Development—Neuroprotective Interventions in Infant–Caregiver Therapy." *Translational Developmental Psychology* 3, no. 1 (2015). doi.org/10.3402/tdp.v3.28647.

O'Brien, Mellissa. "R.A.I.N: A Four-Step Process for Using Mindfulness in Difficult Times." September 13, 2018. mrsmindfulness.com/r-n-four-step-process-using -mindfulness-difficult-times.

Pappas, Stephanie. "Oxytocin: Facts About the 'Cuddle Hormone.'" *Live Science*. June 4, 2015. livescience .com/42198-what-is-oxytocin.html.

Rosabal-Coto, Mariano, Naomi Quinn, Heidi Keller, Marga Vicedo, Nandita Chaudhary, Alma Gottlieb, Gabriel Scheidecker, Marjorie Murray, Akira Takada, and Gilda

A. Morelli. "Real World Applications of Attachment Theory." In *The Cultural Nature of Attachment: Contextualizing Relationships and Development*, edited by Heidi Keller and Kim Bard, 335–54. Cambridge, MA: MIT Press/Frankfurt Institute, 2017. doi.org/10.7551/mitpress/9780262036900.003.0014.

Sasson, Remez. "How Many Thoughts Does Your Mind Think in One Hour?" Accessed October 8, 2019. successconsciousness.com/blog/inner-peace/how-many-thoughts-does-your-mind-think-in-one-hour.

Serani, Deborah. "How Can Feeling Guilty Affect Your Health?" *Sharecare*. Accessed October 8, 2019. sharecare.com/health/human-emotions/how-feeling-guilty-affect-health.

Shpancer, Noam. "Emotional Acceptance: Why Feeling Bad Is Good." *Psychology Today*. September 8, 2010. psychologytoday.com/ca/blog/insight-therapy/201009/emotional-acceptance-why-feeling-bad-is-good.

St. John, Noah. "Why Your Mind Is Like an Iceberg." *HuffPost*. December 7, 2017. huffpost.com/entry/why-your-mind-is-like-an-_b_6285584.

Styron, Thomas. "The Long-Term Effects of Childhood Abuse: An Attachment Theory Perspective." Master's thesis, University of Massachusetts Amherst, 1995. scholarworks.umass.edu/cgi/viewcontent.cgi?article=3423&context=theses.

Taylor, Jane. "6 Core Human Needs by Anthony Robbins." *Habits for Wellbeing*. 2015. https://www.habitsforwellbeing.com/6-core-human-needs-by-anthony-robbins/.

RESOURCES

personaldevelopmentschool.com
The Personal Development School is an online platform
filled with in-depth course material, worksheets, and
resources that will help you transform your attachment style
and enhance your self-healing journey. The courses come
with in-depth tools for subconscious reprogramming, different therapeutic modalities for transformation, and ongoing
webinars and workbooks for results-oriented change.

INDEX

ACKNOWLEDGEMENTS

There are a variety of people that have made this book possible. First, I'd like to thank my sister, Sjorland Gibson, for her support throughout this process. Secondly, I'd like to express gratitude to all the people that have graciously shared their stories and chosen to commit themselves to becoming happier and healthier. It is through the blessing of working with wonderful clients that I have developed the theories and processes that I share in this book. I want to thank my amazing partner, Graham, for his incredible support, care, and wisdom. Last, I want to express gratitude to both of my parents, Melanie and Peter, and my business partner in the Personal Development School, Giovanni, who has been a wonderful friend and kindred spirit.

ABOUT THE AUTHOR

**Thais Gibson** is a lifelong student of the mind, with an MA in transpersonal psychology and more than 10 different certifications in CBT, NLP, hypnosis, and more. She currently runs two successful companies: the Personal Development School and her client-based practice. Throughout her extensive education and career in psychology, she has gathered research that has allowed her to create the techniques described in this book. Drawing from existing theories from a variety of sources, she has been able to combine her experience with well-respected theories to help thousands experience significant life transformations.